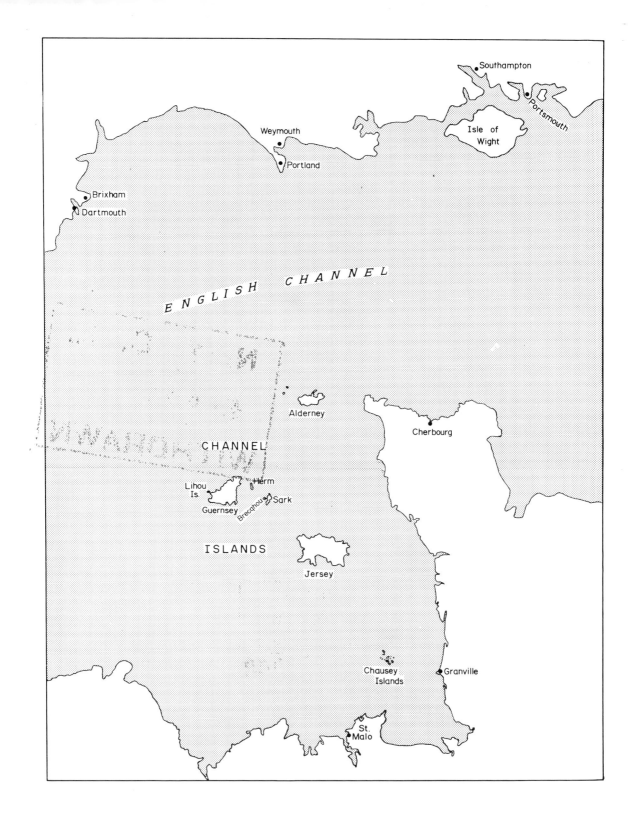

STAMPS AND POSTAL HISTORY OF THE CHANNEL ISLANDS

WILLIAM NEWPORT, F.R.P.S.L.

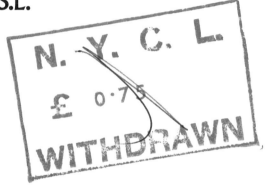

HEINEMANN: LONDON

William Heinemann Ltd
15 Queen St, Mayfair, London W1X 8BE
LONDON   MELBOURNE   TORONTO
JOHANNESBURG   AUCKLAND

Photoset and printed in Great Britain by
BAS Printers Limited, Wallop, Hampshire

PREFACE

The Channel Islands are part of the British Isles but are not part of the United Kingdom. They have had their own forms of government for many centuries, but their major laws are subject to approval by the Queen in Council and they are administered by the Home Office. From 1794 to 1969 they were part of the British postal system and used British forms of postal markings. From 1840 to 1969 they used British postage stamps except for the brief period of the German Occupation from 1940 to 1945, and even then the stamps they produced were issued by British postal officials and were recognized by the Postmaster General; for nearly a year after liberation these stamps remained valid for use on letters addressed to all parts of the world.

The first recorded letter from Jersey is dated 1447 and is addressed to Viscount Beaumont and Lord Sudley from the Bailiff and Jurats. Letters from the sixteenth century onwards are in private hands and can sometimes be obtained by collectors.

There has always been a steady following for Channel Islands stamps and postal markings, and this has grown greatly since the establishment of independent postal services in 1969. For more than twenty years before then, members of the Channel Islands Specialists' Society had been studying the philately of that area. The results of their researches were published in a series of small booklets on specific topics but many of these are now out of print and difficult to acquire.

I was very pleased, therefore, to be approached with the suggestion that the published material should be brought together as one handbook. This work is the result and I have taken the opportunity to revise and up-date previously published matter and to add new sections. It is hoped that the book may create even more collectors of the stamps and postal history of the Channel Islands.

Sidcup, Kent   WILLIAM NEWPORT

ACKNOWLEDGMENTS

As mentioned in the Preface, some of the material included in this book has previously been published in the works of the Channel Islands Specialists' Society and I am very grateful to the many members of the Society who have helped with small pieces of information.

I am particularly grateful to Mr. O. J. Simpson, who has allowed me to use the material which he contributed to some of our joint works and to the Postal History Society and Mr. J. M. Y. Trotter for allowing me to use the list of Letter Forwarding Agents. Mr. Trotter has also kindly provided other information.

My thanks are also due to Richard Mayne; Alan W. Robertson, M.B.E.; Mrs Jean Farrugia, formerly of Post Office Records; the Directors of Posts of Guernsey and Jersey; the Tenants of Herm, Jethou, and Lihou; the Secretary of the Commodore Shipping Company Ltd.; and the Librarians of the Public Library, Jersey, and the Guille-Allès Library, Guernsey, for their assistance.

W. N.

Note
Catalogue numbering in this book is the same as that used in the *Specialised Priced Catalogue of Channel Islands Stamps*, the standard work published by the Channel Islands Specialists' Society. Reference should be made to that *Catalogue* for information on the current prices of stamps which are mentioned herein.

CONTENTS

LIST OF MAPS

Further maps will be found as follows:

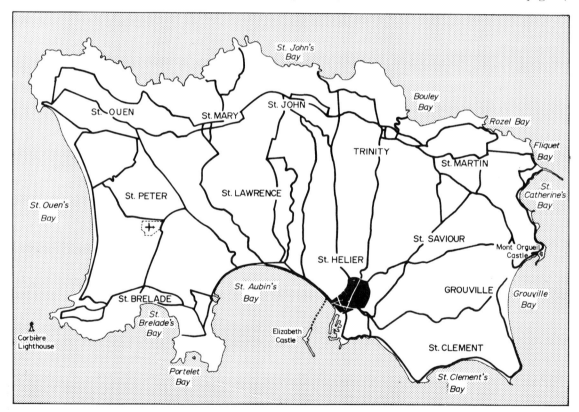

Jersey

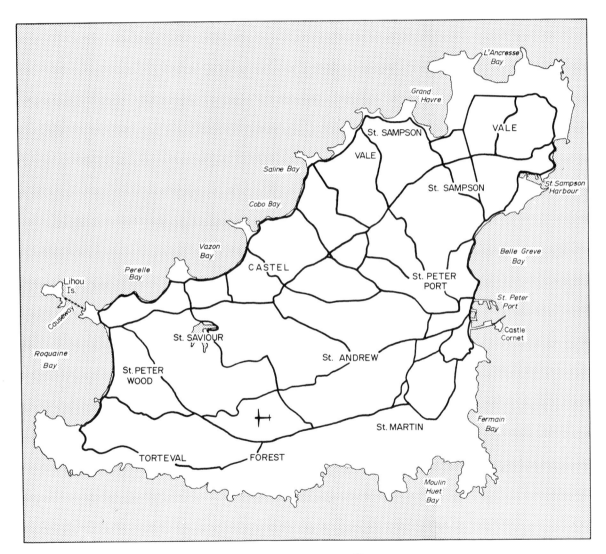

Guernsey

ix

1

LETTER FORWARDING AGENTS

Prior to the establishment of Post Offices in Jersey and Guernsey and a regular packet service to the Islands in 1794, letters for those places were sent to an agent, usually at Southampton, but occasionally at Brixham or Portsmouth, who paid the inland postage and then handed them to the captain of a ship sailing for the Channel Islands. On arrival at Jersey or Guernsey the captain handed over the letter to another agent, from whom they were collected by the addressee upon payment of the British inland postage plus a fee of 3d.—1d. for the ship's master and 1d. for each agent. Letters from the Channel Islands to England were handed over to the Post Office at Southampton by the ship's captain and therefore cost only 2d. on top of the postage.

Most of the agents were merchants but some were also ship owners and one or two shopkeepers or bankers. Many of the London coffee houses also acted as agents and bags for particular ship's captains were often to be found in them.

There were also agents in Bristol, Falmouth, Gosport, Plymouth, Poole, and Weymouth but most of these started up after the packet service was established, and ran in competition with it.

Of the Southampton agents the one doing the largest business in the latter half of the eighteenth century was William Seward who, alone, or with a partner, was an agent for some thirty-seven years, from 1756 to 1793. He charged the usual 1d. except in cases where he had paid more than a shilling postage, when the charge was generally 2d.

Brixham was used as a port for Guernsey mails when the wind was south-westerly, which was directly adverse from the Needles. James Ahier was at work in Weymouth from 1800, and was joined by Nicholas Robilliard in 1802. In the following year Robilliard took

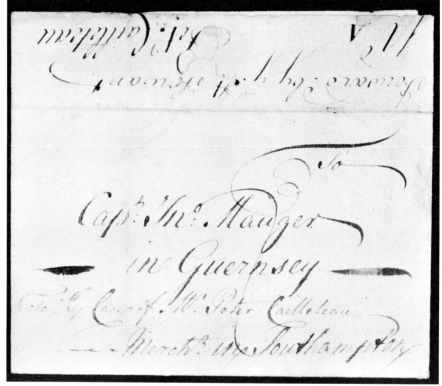

1.1 Agent's endorsement (on flap)

over altogether and carried on until 1810. A considerable quantity of
mail from Britain and overseas went through his hands and it is
suspected that he paid members of the packet crews to smuggle
letters into the Channel Islands for him.

Most of the agents endorsed their letters 'Forwarded by your
humble servant (signature)' (Figure 1.1). A number of them also
added their charge in manuscript, so that one finds the original
inland postage charge crossed out and a higher one substituted; then
the Guernsey or Jersey agent would cross out that figure and add his
own and the captain's penny, writing the final sum to be collected
from the addressee. Letters addressed to local firms were often charged
on account rather than individually. One or two of the early

Southampton agents worked at such cheap rates as ¼d. and ½d., so that one finds letters charged at such curious sums as 3¼d. An oval rubber stamp was struck in blue by N. M. Priaulx, of Southampton, in 1840 (Figure 1.2).

1.2

There were also agents in France and many other European countries and their endorsements can also be found on letters. Mr. J. M. Y. Trotter, of Guernsey, has kindly provided the following list of agents, to which I have added a few whose endorsements appear on letters in my own collection.

Southampton

Caesar Knapton	1673
Grevichy	1689
Aaron Deveule	1703
Bandinell & Co.	1718
Bandinell & Hilgrove	1718–19
Thomas Bandinell	1719–29
John Grove	1713–41
T. Le Cocq	1726
Richard Taunton	1711–33
Bonner	1737–45
Peter Cailleteau	1735–58
Esther Cailleteau & Co.	1758
Clement Hilgrove	1777–79
Hilgrove & Durell	1779–84
Thomas Durell	1786–93
Seward & Marett	1756–58
William Seward	1758–86
Seward & Marett	1756–58
Seward & Le Feuvre	1785–88
Seward & Pipon	1790–93
Seward & Co.	1791–93
P. Le Feuvre	1791–1817
P. Le Feuvre & Son	1818
W. I. Le Feuvre	1820–35
Priaulx & Bienvenu	1796–1812
N. M. Priaulx	1835–40
Helleur	1839

Brixham

John N. Tozer	1738
Samuel Tozer	1793–94
Thomas Parkinson	1781–82

Weymouth

James Ahier	1800–03
Ahier & Robilliard	1802
Nicholas Robilliard	1802–10
Thomas Martin	1803–05
John Sandford Jnr.	1813

Falmouth

George C. Fox & Son	1805
Jos. Banfield	1810

Bristol

Ball, Davis, Vaughan & Co.	1804

Portsmouth

James Wilkinson	1741
John Carey	1812

Gosport

William Carver	1798

Lyme

Henry Chard	1793

Poole

Thomas Nicholson	1723

Plymouth

Noel	1794

London

M. Perchard	1757
Cazelet & Sons	1783
Peyerimhoff, De Mierro & Crispen	1784
Perchard & Brock	1793
Le Mesurier & Secretin	1793
Battier Zornlen	1793–95
Perchard, Brock & Le Mesurier	1798
Brock & Le Mesurier	1805
Wombell, Gautier & Co.	1806
E. Boehm & J. Tayler	1807
Ed. Rodd	1807
Boyd, Miller & Co.	1808
Geo. H. Aylwyn	1810
Fred De Lisle	1811–12
Andrews & Tariner	1812
J. Levy, Jnr.	1815
Jno. McNeill & Co.	1817–18
Bell & Grant	1833–34
Samuel Dobrée & Sons	1834–51

Jersey

Philip Hamond, appointed Postmaster to States	1787
Pierre Mallet	1792
Madame Anne Ashley	1793
Hemery Bros. & Co.	1810
Winter, Nicolle & Co.	1814
J. Le Bailley	1822
Amiraux Le Breton & Co.	1826

P. & I. Danirin	1830
T. & P. Duhamel	1833–35
Godefroy Sons & Co.	1842

Guernsey

Maugher	1718
Mrs. Ann Watson	1780–94
Govt. Postmistress	1794–1814
Harry Dobrée	1810–16
William Lihou	1812
E. Shale	1812
James & John Cochran	1820
Sinclair	1823
Aaron Symes	1828–39
Harris	1828
George S. Syvret & Matthieu Barbet (Foreign P.O.)	1823–41
(also for some years before and after these dates)	
Francis de Putron	1830–37
Edward Le Pelley	1837
Priaulx Langa & Co.	1840

St. Malo

Mace Cohue	1676
J. Monie	1678
Jean Hardy	1682–85
Sebire, Laisne & Cie.	1763
La Dure	1784
Barbier, Robbereckts & Cie.	1802
Louis Blaize & Cie.	1802–23
Louis Blaize	1832
Dupuy, Fromy Frs.	1815–16
J. B. Gaultier	1826–27
Fontan Frs.	1825–30
Mme Veuve Fontan Jun.	1827
Mauger Freres	1827–29
Matthieu Barbet	1829–32

Calais
A. Mancel   1815

Morlaix
P. Aurrere & Fils.   1815
H. Dobrée Jnr.   1816

Le Havre
Charles Sturmer   1814–15

Cherbourg
Captain Poullain   1820–23
J. Boulabert   1823
de Bonfils   1827

Paris
Thomas De Lisle & Co.   1842

Bayonne
Francis Giffard & Son   1815

Alicante
John Carey   1812

Cadiz
R. W. Meade   1812
Gordon, Shaw & Co.   1812

Lisbon
Sealys & Goodall   1813

Naples
Bardon, Maingy & Price   1817–18

Rome
Pierre Meraj   1802

Trieste
J. Janvrin   1822

Gibraltar
Robinson & Lihou   1809
Matthew G. Price   1810
Dobrée, Price & Co.   1811–12
Robert Anderson & Co.   1832

Malta
E. C. Puslow   1815

Bolzano (Botzen)
G. Giacomo Graff   1803

Altona
John Hutchinson   1804

Hamburg
J. B. Paschen & Co.   1793
H. D. Schaffler   1803
J. A. Schroders   1836

Elsinore
Balfour & Rainols   1807

St. Thomas
Bergeert & Ulhorn   1813

Most of the above agents were agents for Guernsey letters, a few were agents for Jersey letters, and a few probably acted as agents for both Islands. As the small trading cutters usually went direct from

Southampton to their own island, it seems that their Southampton agents, goods or postal, were not always the same for each island.

In Guernsey some of the shopkeepers in St. Peter Port acted as agents for letters for private persons in country districts. Persons from the parishes would leave letters in the town to be collected by the addressees. The shops made no charge and there was usually no endorsement of the letters.

2

THE ESTABLISHMENT OF THE POSTAL SERVICE

In the previous chapter it was explained that there was no official postal service to the Channel Islands prior to 1794. For the brief period of five years, from 1778 to 1783, however, there was an attempt to carry mails to the Channel Islands as a war measure and the cutter *Express*, of 40 tons, sailed from Southampton 'as often as practicable.' In 1783 she returned to Dover to continue in service on the Dover–Calais run.

In 1791 the British Government ordered the Postmaster of Southampton to make a census of all letters addressed to the Channel Islands over a period of four weeks, and from this it was deduced that the annual number of letters to be carried would be somewhere around 30,000. On this basis it was considered that a packet service would not be self-supporting, but that, in view of the importance of the Islands during a war with France, such a service should be established as a matter of state.

On February 3, 1794 (and other dates during the month) a notice regarding a packet service to the Channel Islands was published in the *London Gazette* and the first packet, the 80-ton cutter *Royal Charlotte*, sailed from Weymouth for Guernsey on February 13. An Act of Parliament establishing the packet service was passed on March 28, 1794. It also fixed rates of postage and authorized the Postmaster General to establish post offices and post roads in the Islands. The title of the Act was '34 Geo. III, Cap. XVIII (1794).' It was registered by the Royal Court of Guernsey on October 6, 1794, but was never registered by the Royal Court of Jersey and so was not law there.

A Post Office Surveyor, Christopher Saverland, went over on the first packet, and appointed Mrs. Ann Watson Postmistress of Guernsey and Charles William Le Geyt Postmaster of Jersey.

The packet sailed from Weymouth once a week, at first on Thursday evening, but soon afterwards on Saturday evening. In 1807 a twice-weekly service was established and by 1829 there was a thrice-weekly service in the summer months from April to September.

With the *Royal Charlotte* from the beginning was the *Rover*, another Dover packet of 67 tons. In July, 1827, the first two paddle-steamers were put into service and the average time taken for a letter to get to London from the Channel Islands was reduced from five to three days. The packet service continued from Weymouth until 1845, after which letters were carried by private vessels from either Weymouth or Southampton.

The packet rates between Weymouth and the Channel Islands were established in 1794 at 2d. per single letter, 4d. per double letter, 6d. per treble letter, 8d. per ounce letter, and so on in proportion. In November, 1805, they were raised to 3d. per single letter and *pro rata*. The same rates were charged for the inter-island mail between Guernsey and Jersey.

The postage from London to Weymouth in 1794 was 5d., so it cost 7d. to send a letter from London to the Channel Islands. In 1796 it rose to 9d., in 1801 to 10d., in 1805 to 11d. and in 1812 to 1s. 1d. per single letter.

The post office in Jersey was in Hue Street, on the outskirts of the town, but when Le Geyt's son, George William, succeeded him in 1816 it was transferred to a more central position in Minden Place. During the first year of the Jersey post office Le Geyt senior charged an additional 1d. on each letter above the official postage, but this was abolished in 1795, after protests from the States of Jersey, and Le Geyt was given an official allowance to make up his loss.

The inhabitants of St. Aubin employed a private messenger to fetch all their letters and newspapers from the post office once a week after the arrival of the packet. They paid the messenger 1½d. for each letter and 1d. for each newspaper. Later a similar arrangement continued until 1830.

In 1798 Mary Godfray was engaged by Le Geyt to deliver letters in St. Helier. She was the only letter-carrier until 1830 and received no pay, charging ½d. on each letter that she delivered. She sorted her letters into two bundles, which she carried in red and blue handkerchiefs. In 1830 Mary Godfray was paid 6s. a week for two deliveries and five other letter-carriers were engaged. One was paid 6s. a week, and the others 5s., for two deliveries.

The Guernsey post office was in the High Street, just below the arch leading to the Constable's Office. Mrs. Watson, the Postmistress, was succeeded by her son, Nicholas, in 1814.

Two letter-carriers were appointed in 1830: Peter Desperques, aged 30, for the town of St. Peter Port, and Peter Martin, aged 26, for St. Martins and to and from the mailboat. At first they were paid 5s. and 6s. respectively for two deliveries a week. This was later raised to 8s. for a daily delivery.

Guernsey Militia Letters

During the Napoleonic Wars letters from the Guernsey Militia were carried round the Island by the Militia chasseurs. Examples seen range in date from 1790 to 1814. Five dated from 1790 to 1799 are

2.1   Militia letter
of 1795

9

from Headquarters to Colonel Gosselin, Commander of the North Regiment, and contain instructions and official orders (Figure 2.1). One of 1800 is from the Harbour Master to Thomas de Sausmarez and enquires whether a fine has been paid by a ship's captain for not reporting that his vessel had entered harbour. An 1811 letter is from the Inspector of Militia to the Constables of St. Saviour's and refers to the maintenance of beacons and the use of horses and carts in the event of an alarm. The last, dated 1814, is from the Barrack Master and is addressed to Thomas de Sausmarez. All are inscribed 'On Service' on the front. A letter dated 1727 is the earliest seen and is from Louis Dallon, Lieutenant-Governor of Guernsey, ordering Nicolas de Garis, of St. Peter-in-the-Wood, to attend a cavalry muster. It is not marked 'On Service', as are the others described above.

The Head Postmasters

The Head Postmasters from 1794 to September 30, 1969 were:

	GUERNSEY	
From	*To*	
March 27, 1794	June 27, 1814	Mrs. Ann Watson.
June 28, 1814	December 9, 1841	Nicholas Watson.
December 10, 1841	February 17, 1845	William Fell.
February 18, 1845	July 19, 1847	Arthur Forrest.
July 20, 1847	February 6, 1848	Richard Ayre.
February 7, 1848	April 2, 1852	George A. Ross.
April 3, 1852	April 20, 1889	Nicholas Le Messurier.
April 21, 1889	January, 1898	N. Le Messurier Jnr.
January, 1898	August, 1913	P. Le Marinel.
August, 1913	July 11, 1917	J. Matthews.
July 12, 1917	August 7, 1919	Bell Smith.
August 8, 1919	January 27, 1922	H. Roberts.
January 28, 1922	November 14, 1925	J. Pierce.
November 15, 1925	January 30, 1931	J. Harrison.
January 31, 1931	August, 30, 1934	H. Coleman.
August 31, 1934	April, 1937	Captain A. Grist.

August, 1937	June, 1940	W. A. Payne.
June, 1940	December 31, 1956	H. C. Chapell, M.B.E.
January 1, 1957	November 8, 1959	S. F. Child.
January 5, 1960	September 30, 1969	A. G. Williams.

In the period between April and August, 1937, H. J. Cohu was Acting Head Postmaster pending the new appointment. From May 17 to July 6, 1945, H. J. Cohu was in Guernsey as Acting Head Postmaster helping to restore the postal service after liberation. From November 9, 1959, to January 4, 1960, J. J. Spillane was Acting Head Postmaster pending the new appointment.

JERSEY

From	*To*	
February 18, 1794	February 20, 1816	Charles William Le Geyt
February 21, 1816	February 6, 1842	George William Le Geyt
February 7, 1842	April 14, 1843	Arthur Woodgate.
April 15, 1843	February 1, 1848	Robert Fullerton.
February 2, 1848	1855	George Henry Smith.
1855	1869	A. Forrest.
1869	July, 1891	E. Blakeney.
July, 1891	June 22, 1892	F. H. Freeling, Postmaster and Surveyor of Channel Islands.
June 23, 1892	September 20, 1908	J. R. Syvret.
September 21, 1908	May 11, 1915	C. Fenton.
May 12, 1915	July 12, 1919	W. F. Ford.
July 13, 1919	January 2, 1922	A. L. Forrest.
January 3, 1922	March 23, 1927	H. Roberts.
March 24, 1927	October 25, 1933	A. E. Kemp.
October 26, 1933	June, 1940	H. Monks.

June 21, 1940—Alexander M. Coutanche, Bailiff of Jersey, sworn in as Civil Governor. Under his emergency powers he assumed the position of Postmaster-General of Jersey. O. F. Mourant was Acting Head Postmaster.

July 7, 1945	May 1, 1948	O. F. Mourant, M.B.E.
May 2, 1948	June 30, 1959	R. G. Evans.
July 12, 1959	February 8, 1965	J. Anderson.

April 5, 1965   September 30, 1969   L. E. Cockbill

For a short period in 1855 W. Montgomery was Clerk-in-Charge pending the new appointment. From May 17 to July 6, 1945, W. A. Payne was Acting Head Postmaster and representative of the P.M.G. in the Channel Islands, supervising the restoration of the postal service after liberation. From July 1 to July 11, 1959, C. J. d'Authreau was Acting Head Postmaster pending the new appointment.

Locations of the Head Post Offices

GUERNSEY

1794 to 1841	High Street, just by the archway leading to the Le Marchant house, now the Constables' Office. It is now Tylers' Boot Shop.
1841 to 1845	42 Commercial Arcade. Now Fletcher's Sports Shop.
1845 to 1848	16 Fountain Street. Now the Handyman's Stores.
1848 to 1883	36 Commercial Arcade. Now Yvonne's Leather Goods Shop.
May 22, 1883	Smith Street. The present building.

JERSEY

1794 to 1816	Hue Street.
1816 to 1843	Minden Place.
1843 to 1852	9 Bond Street.
1852 to 1881	18 Queen Street.
September 28, 1881 to 1909	Albert Hall (now Mechanics' Institute), Halkett Place.
June, 21, 1909	Broad Street. The present building.

Roadside Letter Boxes

An interesting chapter in the Channel Islands postal history concerns the erection of pillar boxes, or roadside letter boxes as they were then called. In November, 1852, the first letter boxes in the United Kingdom were erected experimentally in Jersey at the instance of Anthony Trollope, the novelist. Trollope was a Post Office surveyor and his district at that time included the Channel Islands. It is believed that he got the idea of letter boxes from France, where they had been in use for several years.

A Jersey Post Office Notice of November, 1852, stated that on and after November 23 roadside letter boxes would be opened for collecting public correspondence in David Place, New Street, Cheapside, and St. Clement's Road.

Three boxes were erected in Guernsey in 1853. A Post Office Notice in the *Star* and *Comet* of February 10 stated that boxes had been opened from February 8 at Hauteville, Union Street, and The Piette. The boxes were numbered 1, 2, and 3. No. 1 was situated at 12 Union Street, No. 2 at 5 Hauteville, and No. 3 at The Piette. Three more boxes were erected later in 1853 at Colborne Place, Choisi, and Elm Grove.

None of the Jersey boxes now remains but two of the Guernsey boxes were standing in 1952 when the centenary of the Channel Islands boxes was celebrated. The Hauteville box (Figure 2.2) was replaced by a modern one in February, 1953, and was presented to the States of Guernsey Ancient Monuments Committee, who presented it to the British Post Office in 1969. The Union Street box is still in use, and a special cancellation was applied to letters posted in it on February 9, 1970.

The success of Trollope's experiment is proved by the fact that there are now 90,000 pillar, wall, and 'lamp-post' boxes in use in Britain today.

2.2 The Hauteville box. It now stands outside Mercury House, Headquarters of the South West Postal Region, Market Place, Bristol, following presentation to the British Post Office.

THE EARLY POSTAL MARKINGS

3.1

3.2 Type 2

3.3 Type 1

3.4 Type 2

The first postal marking in use in Jersey and Guernsey consisted of the name of the island in a concave curve (Figures 3.1 and 3.2). In Jersey there was a single stamp in use from 1794 to 1798 but in Guernsey there were three types used between 1794 and 1810. Type 1 measures 46mm wide and was used from 1794 to 1801; type 2 measures 49mm wide and was used from 1802 to 1807; type 3 measures 37mm wide and was used from 1808 to 1810. All examples seen of type 3 are very faintly impressed.

In Jersey from 1797 to 1810 a straight-line stamp was in use which can be found in two different types. Type 1 measures 32 × 5mm, has a full loop to the J and wide letters (Figure 3.3). It was used from 1797 to 1806; type 2 measures 30 × 5mm, has no top bar to the J and over the years the loop at the bottom almost disappeared (Figure 3.4). In some examples there appears to be a small dot over the J making it look like an I. It was used from 1807 to 1810 and was re-used in 1829–30.

From 1810 both islands used the well-known scroll stamps. In Jersey a type having oval loops, the J close to the edge of the frame and a full stop after JERSEY was used from 1810 to 1817 and 1822–30 (Figure 3.5). A second type with rounder loops, the J further from the edge of the frame and no stop after JERSEY was used from 1817 to 1830 (Figure 3.6).

Two types were also used in Guernsey. The first (Figure 3.7) with oval loops, the G close to the edge of the frame and a full stop after GUERNSEY, was used from 1810 to 1817 and is also known struck on telegraph forms in 1870–72, so although taken out of use in 1817 it must have survived until at least 1872 and may still be in existence somewhere. The second type (Figure 3.8) with rounder loops, the G further from the edge of the frame and no stop after GUERNSEY, was used from 1817 to 1830.

A Penny Post was established in Jersey in 1830, running between the chief town and the parishes. A special handstamp (Figure 3.9) was used from 1831 to 1838 and small handstamps No. 1, No. 2, No. 3, No. 4, No. 5, and No. 6 in boxes are believed to have been issued to Gorey, St. Aubin, St. Clement's, St. Peter's, St. Saviour's, and Trinity. Nos. 1 and 2 are known and have been identified as being used at St. Aubin and Gorey respectively. Nos. 3 and 4 were almost certainly used at St. Peter's and St. Clement's. The handstamps are illustrated at Figures 3.9(*a*)–(*d*). The other numbers have not yet been seen. The Guernsey Penny Post was established between January and March, 1836. No Guernsey Penny Post handstamps have yet been found, although La Valle and Torteval are recorded by Hendy as being served by it.

One other pre-adhesive mark can be recorded. In Jersey in 1831 a 'too late' handstamp in lower-case letters (Figure 3.10) was used on letters for London posted too late to catch the mailboat.

Refer to Chapter 8 for other pre-adhesive markings (on letters arriving in France from the Channel Islands).

Ship Letters

The Act of 1794 establishing post offices in Jersey and Guernsey brought these offices into the Post Office system and therefore subject to English Parliamentary Acts. But the States of Jersey and Guernsey were independent legislatures and English Acts transmitted to the Islands by the Privy Council were not legally binding until registered by the Royal Court of the Island.

In the rest of the United Kingdom, letters landed from private ships were subject to the enacted ship letter charges. These charges now became payable to the Post Office on letters landed at Jersey and

3.5

3.6

3.7

3.8

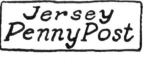

3.9

3.9(a)	3.9(b)	3.9(c)	3.9(d)
St. Aubin	Gorey	Probably St. Peter's	Probably St. Clement's

too late

3.10

Guernsey. The President's Order Book of 1794, in Post Office Records, records for August 15 the ordering of a ship letter stamp for Jersey. This would be the two-line type JERSEY/SHIP LRE. No example has yet been seen.

In 1799 the Ship Letter Office (with revised and new procedures

3.11

3.12 Only known example of Jersey oval ship letter

SHIP

3.13

relating to ship letters) was established in London with the necessary Parliamentary enactment. A new type of ship letter handstamp, the double-oval and crown, replaced the previous two-line 'Ship Lre' handstamps. The second form of this oval began to be issued in 1802 and an example was sent to Guernsey (Figure 3.11). It had two periods of use, from 1802 to 1815 and from 1844 to 1849. The pay-

16

ment of ship letter charges was strenuously opposed in the Channel Islands because most of the letters taken in by ship to the Islands were carried by vessels belonging to local owners, returning to their home ports from overseas. The letters were mainly for local citizens and to have to pay a levy on such letters was regarded by the islanders as iniquitous. Very few letters were therefore handed over to the Post Office by the masters of incoming vessels and the oval Guernsey ship letter stamp lay idle for most of its life. Only about five examples of this strike now exist. The only Jersey example of the oval ship letter is on a letter of 1808 in the Joseph Banks correspondence in the British Museum (Figure 3.12).

A letter from Stapehill, near Wimborne, Dorset, to Jersey of June 8, 1828, has a small handstruck mark SHIP, measuring 9mm long by 3mm high, in black serifed letters (Figure 3.13). The postage paid is inscribed 10d. Further enquiries are being made as to its status.

In 1834 the boxed types of ship letter stamps (Figures 3.14 and 3.15) were sent to both islands. They are by far the commonest Channel Islands types and are usually found on letters carried from Rio de Janeiro and Bahia, from whence there were frequent sailings of fast vessels carrying coffee to Le Havre. The English mails, mainly addressed to Huth and Rothschild of London, were dropped off at Jersey or Guernsey and received the ship letter marks of those ports. The Jersey stamp was used until 1843. The Guernsey one was used

GUERNSEY SHIP LETTER	JERSEY SHIP LETTER
3.14	3.15

until 1842 when it was replaced by the rare step type (Figure 3.16) which was in use for a few months only and only about four examples are known.

An unusual type for both islands is one similar to the 1834 boxed stamp but with the lettering transposed and struck in red (Figures 3.17 and 3.18). About eight examples of the Guernsey stamp exist and two Jersey. The Guernsey stamps are dated 1836–40 and the Jersey stamps are dated 1836–37. All are on letters from Brazil to a

GUERNSEY SHIP LETTER

3.16 Rare step type of 1842

SHIP LETTER GUERNSEY

3.17

SHIP LETTER JERSEY

3.18

JERSEY SHIP-LETTER

3.19

London banking firm. There are strong reasons for believing that these stamps were applied in London to letters for the same address which were bundled in Rio and passed through the Guernsey and Jersey post offices intact. In London the bundles would be opened and the red Guernsey or Jersey ship letter stamp applied to each letter. It is unlikely that either Jersey or Guernsey would have had two ship letter stamps in use in the 1830s and, in any case, red ink pads were not in use in the islands at that time. The ink used for the ship letters does, however, match that used for applying the London circular datestamps of that period.

In Jersey an unframed type (Figure 3.19) was in use from 1843 to 1853. It was usually struck in black but examples of it are known in blue in 1851 and yellow in 1852.

On the single known example of the cover bearing the blue stamp, an entire from Anchor Point, Newfoundland, to Parkstone, near Poole, Dorset, is a handstruck 8 in blue. Although quite a number of covers from this correspondence are known, only one has the ship letter in blue and the handstruck 8; on all the others the 8d. charge is in manuscript.

Guernsey had an India Letter handstamp (Figure 3.20): a single example is known applied in 1836 on a letter from Singapore.

Letters from overseas with Jersey or Guernsey scrolls or datestamps are not really ship letters but were brought in by ship and handed over to private agents who posted them 'illegally' as though they were ordinary letters written in the islands, thus evading the ship letter charge.

THE PENNY SHIP LETTER RATE

The railway reached Southampton in June, 1840, and the run between London and Southampton could be accomplished in about three hours. The Post Office thereupon granted permission for letters to be sent to and from the Channel Islands via Southampton instead of via Weymouth, providing that they were endorsed 'Via Southampton by Private Steamer.' This soon became abbreviated to 'Per Southampton' or 'Per Steamer.'

Letters from the Channel Islands received the current Southampton Ship Letter handstamp and those addressed to the Channel

```
┌─────────────────────────┐
│  INDIA LETTER           │
│    GUERNSEY             │
│                         │
└─────────────────────────┘
```
3.20   One example known, 1836

Islands often received the red oval London Paid Ship Letter date-stamp. They were charged at the normal domestic rate of 1d. per $\frac{1}{2}$oz instead of the 8d. charged on ship letters from overseas.

This service enabled letters posted in time to catch a vessel going to Southampton one morning to be delivered in London the next morning, against the three days taken by the service by packet to Weymouth and then by road to London. The packet service was, however, still advantageous for letters addressed to the West Country, which the railway had not reached, and continued to function until 1845.

THE CHANNEL ISLANDS—PLYMOUTH SERVICE

From about 1823 the 170-ton paddle steamer *Sir Francis Drake* ran a regular summer service between Plymouth and the Channel Islands. She left Stonehouse Pool at 4.30 p.m. every Thursday afternoon, arriving in Guernsey the next morning and then going on to Jersey. She left Jersey at noon and Guernsey at 5 p.m. every Friday on the homeward journey. She was owned by William Langdown, a merchant of 12 Union Street, Stonehouse. The Channel Islands agents were J. B. Barbet (Guernsey) and John Benest (Jersey).

From 1840 the Postmaster General allowed letters to be carried on this service at the domestic postage rate of 1d. The letters were either given to the purser or posted in a box on board and on arrival at their destination were cancelled by the post office of the port concerned. Thus letters from the Channel Islands would be cancelled at Plymouth and those from Plymouth would be cancelled at Jersey or Guernsey.

In the Société Jersiaise Museum at St. Helier is an 1850 cover from Plymouth to Jersey with the postage stamp cancelled with the unframed Jersey Ship Letter handstamp. The cover is endorsed 'P Drake.' A loose 1d. red stamp is also known with the same cancellation.

In July, 1858, the *Sir Francis Drake* was replaced by the iron clipper steamship *Sir Walter Raleigh* and I have an entire carried by this vessel from Guernsey which has the 1d. red stars stamp cancelled in blue with the 620 duplex cancellation of October 16, 1858. It is endorsed 'Raleigh.'

THE 'FROM GUERNSEY' HANDSTAMP

FROM GUERNSEY

3.21

The Act of 1794 established the packet letter rate at 2d. per single letter. Charges on letters from overseas were much higher; therefore letters to Weymouth carried on the incoming packet, if they bore no Jersey or Guernsey handstruck marks, needed some form of identification to signify that they were from the Channel Islands and, therefore, entitled to be treated as packet letters and not as ship letters. A handstamp reading 'FROM GUERNSEY' (Figure 3.21) was therefore used at Weymouth to mark such letters known to have come from the Channel Islands packet. The stamp was used from 1812 to 1837 and is known on letters from both Guernsey and Jersey. Guernsey being the last port of call on the homeward journey, it was found convenient to mark all the letters as being from Guernsey instead of having handstamps inscribed for both islands.

SOUTH COAST SHIP LETTER STAMPS ON C.I. MAIL

Letters from the Channel Islands were often brought into this country by private ships and when handed over to the Post Office received the ship letter stamp of the port of arrival. The following types are known (numbers according to Alan Robertson's *Maritime Postal History of the British Isles*): *Southampton*, S1, S2, S3, S4, (black and red), S6, S7, S7a, S10 (black and red), S11, S12 (black and blue); *Portsmouth*, S11, S15; *Weymouth*, S2, S4; *Plymouth*, S5, S6a; *London*, S51; *Devonport*, S2a.

The ship letter stamps of other ports probably also exist on Channel Islands letters but have not yet been seen. Those that are likely to turn up are Brixham, Bristol, and Falmouth. There were regular services between the first two ports and the Channel Islands in the 1830s, and it is known that Channel Islands letters were sometimes landed at Falmouth. There was also a regular service to London, so earlier London ship letters stamps may also be found.

The Channel Islands Packets

Included in this list are ships which regularly carried mail to and from the Channel Islands after 1845, when Post Office contracts were awarded to Railway Companies operating cross-channel services.

An interesting early shipping notice regarding a service from Poole to Jersey is shown in Figure 3.22 by courtesy of Mr. Alan Robertson.

POST OFFICE SAILING PACKETS

(The packet service between Weymouth and the Channel Islands commenced with the establishment of Channel Islands Post Offices in 1794.)

Name	Built	Rig	Tonnage	Service
Royal Charlotte	—	Cutter	80	Weymouth–Channel Islands
Rover	1794	Cutter	67	,, ,, ,,
Earl of Chesterfield	1795	Cutter	78	,, ,, ,,
Chesterfield	1806	Cutter	80	,, ,, ,,
Francis Freeling	1811	Cutter	80	,, ,, ,,
Hinchinbrook	1811	Cutter	80	,, ,, ,,

Note: the Royal Charlotte was replaced by the Earl of Chesterfield in June, 1795.

POST OFFICE STEAM PACKETS

(Weymouth–Channel Islands steamer service commenced July, 1827. Packets transferred to Admiralty 1837. Service ended 1845.)

Name	Built	Rig	Tonnage	
Ivanhoe	1819	Paddle-steamer	158	(Built for City of Dublin Steam Packet Co.)
Cuckoo	1824	,, ,,	234	(Late *Cinderella* of Irish packet service.)
Flamer	1831	,, ,,	165	(Renamed *Fearless* by Admiralty 1837.)
Meteor	1821	,, ,,	190	(Sank off Portland Bill in 1830.)
Watersprite	1826	,, ,,	162	(Renamed *Wildfire* by Admiralty 1837.)
Pluto	1831	,, ,,	396	(Relief packet not in regular service.)
Dasher	1837	,, ,,	275	(Became Channel Islands Fishery Protection vessel.)

LONDON TO THE CHANNEL ISLANDS

Via POOLE, in TWELVE HOURS,

→ **WITH A BAG OF LETTERS FROM H. M. POST OFFICE.** ←

Passengers and Baggage via POOLE avoid Dock and Pier Dues.

Freight and Rail Charges same as via Southampton.

Goods by this route are free of Dock and Pier Dues.---

Alteration of Time on and after Aug. 1.

THE NEW
STEAM
COMPANY'S

SOUTH-WESTERN
NAVIGATION
UNRIVALLED

STEAM   SHIPS,

Will Leave POOLE HARBOUR,

WITH GOODS AND PASSENGERS, FOR

GUERNSEY & JERSEY

Every MONDAY and THURSDAY Nights, at ELEVEN o'Clock,
Immediately after the arrival of the Up Mail Train from Dorchester;
Returning from JERSEY, every WEDNESDAY Afternoon, at Three o'clock,
and SATURDAY Morning, at Eight o'clock.

The Passage to or from POOLE and GUERNSEY will not exceed **FIVE HOURS AND A HALF,**
THEREBY OFFERING TO THE PUBLIC,
THE MOST RAPID COMMUNICATION BETWEEN THE CHANNEL ISLANDS AND THE METROPOLIS.

FARES to and from LONDON to GUERNSEY and JERSEY, the same as via SOUTHAMPTON, viz:—
**First Class Rail & Main Cabin, 35s. 6d.—Second Class Rail & Main Cabin, 31s. 6d.
Second Class Rail and Second Cabin, 24s. 6d.—Third Class Rail and
Second Cabin, 20s. 8d.**
BETWEEN POOLE AND GUERNSEY AND JERSEY,—
Main Cabin, 21s.—Fore Cabin, 14s.—Carriages, £3.—Horses, £3.—Dogs, 5s.
STEWARD'S FEES.—Main Cabin, 1s.—Fore Cabin, 6d.
1 Cwt. of Personal Baggage is allowed each Chief Cabin Passenger, all above that weight will be charged 6d. per cubic foot.

PASSENGERS EMBARK AND DISEMBARK AT POOLE FREE OF CHARGE.

Goods by the Company's Vessels are carried at very Reduced Rates.
To Merchants and Shippers this route offers peculiar ADVANTAGES OVER EVERY OTHER PORT.
*Merchandize of every description may be Imported or Exported at the low local rate of 3d. per ton only, while the
facilities are equal to any Port in the United Kingdom.*

THE COMPANY'S VESSELS LEAVE

JERSEY FOR ST. MALO,

*Every TUESDAY Afternoon, returning every WEDNESDAY Morning,
at Ten o'clock. Also, from*

JERSEY TO GRANVILLE,

Every FRIDAY Afternoon, returning every SATURDAY Morning,
ACCORDING TO TIDE.

The SOUTH-WESTERN RAILWAY COMPANY'S TRAINS leave POOLE for DORCHESTER, Five times daily—
from whence Fast Coaches start for BRIDPORT, YEOVIL, TAUNTON, EXETER, &c., &c.
Also, from POOLE first-rate Conveyances for BLANDFORD, SHAFTESBURY, BATH, BRISTOL, &c., &c.
*THE NEW SOUTH-WESTERN STEAM NAVIGATION COMPANY will not be responsible for any damage
or loss of Baggage, nor for Delays, Accidents, or Sea Risks of any kind whatsoever.*

New South-Western Steam Navigation Company's Office,   **JOHN BROUGHTON, Agent.**
162, High Street, Poole, July 27th, 1848.

LANKESTER, PRINTER, 91, HIGH STREET, POOLE.

PRIVATELY OWNED PADDLE-STEAMERS PERMITTED BY POST OFFICE TO CARRY MAIL

(As from June, 1840, providing letters were endorsed 'Per Private Steamer.')

Name	Built	Tonnage	Service
Ariadne	1824	197	Southampton–Channel Islands–France.
Lord Beresford	1824	160	Southampton–Channel Islands–France.
Sir Francis Drake	1823	170	Plymouth–Channel Islands.
Brunswick	1825	218	Southampton–Channel Islands.
Bristol	1823	130	Channel Islands–France
Lady de Saumarez	1835	350	Southampton–Channel Islands–France.
Atalanta	1835	315	Southampton–Channel Islands–France
Transit	1835	201	Southampton–Channel Islands.
Sir Walter Raleigh	1858	—	Plymouth–Channel Islands.

STEAMERS OWNED BY RAILWAY COMPANIES, CARRYING MAIL UNDER POST OFFICE CONTRACT AFTER 1845

(A. Paddle-steamers)

Name	Built	Tonnage	Service
Calpi★	1835	131	Southampton–Channel Islands.
Monarch	1836	360	,, ,,
South Western★	1843	204	,, ,,
Transit★	1843	201	,, ,,
Wonder★	1844	250	,, ,,
Dispatch	1847	314	,, ,,
Express	1847	311	,, ,,
Courier	1847	314	,, ,,
Aquila	1854	264	Weymouth–Channel Islands.
Cygnus	1854	245	,, ,,
Alliance	1855	311	Jersey–St. Malo–Gonville
Havre	1856	350	Southampton–Channel Islands.
Brighton	1856	286	Weymouth–Channel Islands.
Fanny	1859	635	Southampton–Channel Islands.
Southampton	1860	460	,, ,,
Normandy	1863	600	,, ,,
Waverley	1864	—	,, ,,
Brittany	1864	529	Southampton–Channel Islands. (After 1873).

B

(B. Screw propulsion)

Name	Built	Tonnage	Service
Caesarea	1867	280	Southampton–Channel Islands.
Guernsey	1874	572	,, ,,
Ella	1881	851	,, ,,
Hilda	1882	849	,, ,,
Honfleur	1873	429	Southampton–Channel Islands–France.
Diana	1877	—	Southampton–Channel Islands.
Laura	1885	641	,, ,,
Lynx	1889	609	Weymouth–Channel Islands.
Antelope	1889	609	,, ,,
Gazelle	1889	613	,, ,,
Dora	1889	820	Southampton–Channel Islands.
Frederica	1890	1,059	,, ,,
Lydia	1890	1,059	,, ,,
Stella	1890	1,059	,, ,,
Ibex	1891	951	Weymouth–Channel Islands.
Roebuck	1897	1,093	,, ,,
Reindeer	1897	1,101	,, ,,
Vera	1898	1,008	Southampton–Channel Islands.
Alberta	1900	1,193	,, ,,
Great Western	1902	1,224	Weymouth–Channel Islands†
Great Southern	1902	1,224	,, ,, †
Princess Ena	1906	1,198	Jersey–France.
Normannia	1910	1,560	Southampton–Channel Islands–Havre.
Caesarea	1910	1,504	Southampton–Channel Islands.
Sarnia	1910	1,504	Southampton–Channel Islands.
Lorina	1918	1,578	Southampton–Channel Islands–Havre.
St. Helier	1925	1,952	Weymouth–Channel Islands.
St. Julien	1925	1,952	,, ,,
Isle of Jersey	1930	2,143	Southampton–Channel Islands.
Isle of Guernsey	1930	2,143	,, ,,
Isle of Sark	1932	2,211	,, ,,
Hantonia	1912	1,594	Southampton–Channel Islands for a short period after World War II.
Brittany	1933	1,522	Jersey–Guernsey; Jersey–St. Malo; Southampton–Channel Islands.
Falaise	1947	3,710	Southampton–Channel Islands.

St. David	1947	3,352	Weymouth–Channel Islands, late 1947.
St. Patrick	1948	3,482	Weymouth–Channel Islands.
Normannia	1952	3,543	Southampton–Channel Islands during winter from 1959; Weymouth–Channel Islands, early 1960.
Caesarea	1960	4,174	Weymouth–Channel Islands, 1961.
Sarnia	1960	4,174	Weymouth–Channel Islands, 1961.

★Wooden built, rest iron.   †Summer months only.

LOCAL CHANNEL ISLANDS MAIL–CARRYING VESSELS

Name	Built	Type	Service
Serpent	c.1850	Screw steamer	Guernsey–St. Malo.
Rose	c.1854	Screw steamer	Jersey–St. Malo.
Fawn	c.1854–94	Cutter	Guernsey–St. Malo–Brieux.
L'Echo	1873–84	Cutter	Guernsey–St. Malo.–Brieux.
Commerce	1874–82	Screw steamer	Guernsey–Jersey–St. Brieux.
Courier	1883–1940	Screw steamer	Guernsey–Alderney–Cherbourg.
Oenone	1885–87	Dandy	Guernsey–St. Malo–St. Brieux.
Fawn	1897–1923	Screw steamer	Guernsey–St. Malo–St. Brieux.
New Fawn	1923–40	Screw steamer	Guernsey–St. Malo–St. Brieux.
Devonia	20th Cent.	Steamer	Plymouth–Guernsey–Jersey–Brieux. (Weekly).

Other local mail-carrying vessels were:

Little Courier, Riduna, Staffa, which carried mails between Guernsey, Alderney, and Sark in the period 1910–58 approximately. Also the following vessels which carried mail between Guernsey and Sark: *Alert, Serk, Helper, Joybell I, Joybell II, Joybell III, White Heather, M.F.V. 1502, Sark Coast, Herm Coast, Red Commodore, White Commodore, Silver Commodore, Fleet Commodore, Commodore Queen, Kyang, Torbay Belle, Merry Golden Hind, Radcliffe, Lady Patricia.* These names were supplied by Mr. Victor Coysh of Guernsey.

The motor launch *Celia* carried mail between Herm and Guernsey during the tenancy of Sir Percival Perry, and the *Arrowhead* and *Henry Rose II* have done so during the tenancy of Major A. G. Wood. Other motor launches have also carried mail between these two islands from time to time.

Wrecks

The rocks and currents around the Channel Islands are very treacherous and many fine ships have been wrecked there. From many of these, mails have been recovered but in only one case is there any record of the letters having been marked in any way and that concerns mail from the s.s. *Ibex* during her second wrecking in 1900.

The *Ibex* left Weymouth on January 4, 1900, and struck a rock in the east channel on the Little Russel, near the Platte Fougère, at 6 a.m. on January 5. One sailor was lost but all the passengers were saved. Forty-four bags of mail went down with the vessel but as she rested on an even keel, with masts, funnels, and part of the superstructure above water at low tide, divers were able to start work on her straight away and two parcel hampers were salvaged on the day of the sinking.

On January 9 the *Star*, a Guernsey newspaper, reported that the mail bags were found to be floating under the poop deck. Five had been recovered by this date, three for Guernsey and two for Jersey. The letters were in fair condition but the newspapers were reported to be pulp. The Guernsey letters were dried and delivered on the 9th, postmen being instructed to explain that they were from the *Ibex*. Salvage continued and by the 12th, thirty-three mail-bags had been recovered.

By January 20 all the mail-bags except two had been recovered. One was from London to Jersey and one from Dorchester to Guernsey. On January 25 the *Star* reported that a bag of mail from the *Ibex* had been washed ashore at St. Brelade's Bay, Jersey.

Letters for Jersey, Alderney, and Sark recovered from the wreck were, after drying, tied up in bundles, or put into envelopes with a manuscript note to say where they had come from

No handstamps were used at Guernsey to identify these letters. Nevertheless, two slightly different cachets reading: 'MAIL PER S.S. IBEX' are known. Both types are 40mm long with letters from printer's type, but one has all the letters 3mm high (except the 'ER' of 'PER' which are 2½mm) and full stops after the 's.s.', while the other has the words 'MAIL' and 'IBEX' in letters 3mm high and 'PER SS' in letters of 2½mm and no stops after 'SS' (Figures 3.23 (a) and (b)).

About nine covers are known with these cachets and all are addressed to Jersey; it would appear, therefore, that the cachets were applied by the Jersey Post Office after the letters were received from Guernsey, or possibly to letters washed up off Jersey.

A news-wrapper in my collection from the magazine *Commerce* addressed to Jersey has in manuscript 'Recovered from wreck of G.W. Rly. s.s. Ibex lost off Guernsey about 28/12/99—received 14/1/1900.' It bears the first type of *Ibex* cachet with small 'ER' of 'PER' and stops after the 's.s.', and so do the other entires delivered around this date. One is known with the Jersey datestamp of January 12, 1900. The later covers, however, with Jersey datestamps of July 30 and August 1, 1900, have the second type of cachet with small 'PER SS' and no stops after the 'SS.' A possible explanation of this is that a further bag of letters was found in the *Ibex* after she had been taken into St. Peter Port on July 21, having in some miraculous way been preserved from the ravages of the sea, and when these letters were delivered in Jersey a new cachet had to be made, the earlier one having been destroyed some months before when it was thought unlikely that any further letters would be recovered.

One of the later covers is a piece of French postal stationery with impressed 5c. green Peace and Commerce stamp cancelled at Le Havre on December 31, 1899. It has an 'officially sealed' label bearing the Jersey datestamp of July 30, 1900, and the second type of *Ibex* cachet. Another cover with this cachet is illustrated in Figure 3.24. This cover also has Jersey arrival stamps of August 1 and 2, 1900.

A list of mailboat wrecks follows. It is not claimed that it is complete, but it will assist readers in their searches for other wreck covers.

Royal Charlotte, steam yacht, 91 tons, lost in gale off Cap la Hogue in October, 1823. Mails?

Rover, cutter, 80 tons, Weymouth–Channel Islands mailboat, wrecked off Alderney, in 1825. Mails?

MAIL PER S.S. IBEX

3.23(a) First type

MAIL PER S S IBEX

3.23(b) Second type

3.24 Cover bearing Type 2 cachet

Hinchinbrook, cutter, 80 tons, wrecked near Longy, Alderney, February 2, 1826, on voyage to Guernsey. Mails saved and brought to Guernsey by the *Experiment*. *Hinchinbrook* a total wreck.

Francis Freeling, cutter, 80 tons, lost in gale September 6, 1826, on voyage Weymouth to Guernsey; probably run down by Swedish brig; no survivors, mails lost.

Experiment, cutter, wrecked on voyage Guernsey to Alderney, March 16, 1850. Mails salved and sent on to Alderney.

South Western Steam Navigation Company's paddle-steamer *Express* ran on rock near Corbière, Jersey, on voyage Jersey to Guernsey, September 30, 1859. Vessel total wreck, mails salved.

Paris, 350 tons, paddle-steamer, wrecked outside St. Helier, July, 1863.

L. & S.W.R. iron paddle-steamer *Normandy*, sank in collision with s.s. *Mary* in fog off Needles, March 17, 1870. Mails not salved.

L. & S.W.R. *Waverley*, iron paddle-steamer, wrecked in fog on rock in Little Russell, Guernsey, May 5, 1873. Mails probably lost.

L. & S.W.R. paddle-steamer *Havre*, wrecked in Little Russell, Guernsey, February 15, 1875. Mails probably lost.

L. & S.W.R. *Caledonia*, 355-ton iron screw steamer, wrecked on rock off St. Helier, Jersey, on February 19, 1881, on voyage Guernsey to Jersey. Mails salved by divers.

L. & S.W.R. *Caesarea* sank in collision with s.s. *Strathesk* in fog 12 miles off Cap la Hogue, June 27, 1884, on voyage Southampton to St. Malo. Mails lost?

Weymouth & Channel Islands Steam Packet Company's *Brighton*, iron paddle-steamer, 286 tons, wrecked on rock in Little Russell, Guernsey, in thick fog, January 29, 1887. Mails lost.

L. & S.W.R. *Lydia*, steel twin-screw steamer, 1,059 tons, struck rock off Fort Doyle, north of Guernsey, May 6, 1891, in fog, but managed to reach harbour in sinking condition. Mails transferred to *Gazelle*.

L. & S.W.R. *Diana*, 850 gross tons, wrecked in 1895 (place not mentioned). Mails, if any, lost.

G.W.R. *Ibex*, steel twin-screw steamer, 951 tons, beached after striking rock near Corbière, Jersey, during race against L. & S.W.R. *Frederica*, April 16, 1897. Mails salved, ship refloated and put back into service.
Again sunk off St. Sampson's, Guernsey, January 5, 1900. Mails salved, ship again raised and put back into service.

L. & S.W.R. *Stella*, wrecked on Casquets, March 30, 1899, afternoon in fog, on voyage Southampton to Guernsey. Mails, if any, lost.

L. & S.W.R. *Hilda*, 850 gross tons, wrecked in blizzard off island of Czembre, near St. Malo, November 18, 1905. Mails, if any, lost.

G.W.R. *Roebuck*, wrecked on Kaines Rocks, off St. Brelades Bay, on July 19, 1911. Mails?

L. & S.W.R. *Guernsey*, 572 tons, wrecked off Cap la Hogue, April 9, 1915. Mails?

L. & S.W.R. *Caesarea*, triple-screw steamer, sank off St. Helier after striking Noirmont Rock, July 7, 1923. Mails?

L. & S.W.R. *Princess Ena*, twin-screw turbine steamer, caught fire and sank on passage from Jersey to St. Malo, August 3, 1935.

The Handstruck Penny and Twopenny Stamps

Uniform Penny Postage commenced on January 10, 1840, and from that day handstruck 1d. paid and 2d. unpaid marks (as well as higher values) were used throughout the British Isles. Nearly every town had its own designs, which were probably made locally. The handstruck 1d. stamps were used concurrently with the adhesives (first issued May 6, 1840) up to 1853 when the use of the latter was made compulsory.

3.25 Jersey,   **3.26** Guernsey,
1844–48   1843–46

3.27(a) Jersey, **3.27(b)** Jersey,
1842–43   1849, 1851

3.27(c) Jersey, **3.27(d)** Jersey,
1852, 1866–67   1853

Both Jersey and Guernsey had their peculiar types. Robson Lowe in his *Encyclopaedia of British Empire Postage Stamps*, vol. 1, records a 1d. type similar to his standard type J used in 1843 and K used in 1847. Type M was used in 1848. Other examples recorded by the Channel Islands Specialists' Society are as Figure 3.25, used in Jersey from 1844 to 1848. In Guernsey a 1d. as Figure 3.26 was used from 1843 to 1846. Being paid stamps, all the 1d.'s were struck in red.

At least four 2d. stamps were used in Jersey. Figure 3.27(a) was used in 1842–43 and was struck in black. Figure 3.27(b) is known in black on a letter of 1849 and in blue on a letter dated September 21, 1851. Figure 3.27(c) is known in blue in June, 1852, and in black in 1866–67. Figure 3.27(d) is known in black in 1847–53.

Two 2d. stamps were used in Guernsey. Figure 3.28(a) is known used in 1842–43 and Figure 3.28(b) in 1847. Both were struck in black.

From the early 1870s handstruck 2d. and 4d. marks of a standard pattern were in use throughout the British Isles and examples are known used in the Channel Islands, as are ½d. and 1d. types issued in the 1880s. These were used up to the issue of adhesive postage-due labels in 1914.

In Jersey a blue '8' (Figure 3.29) was used to collect ship letter charges in 1851.

A large handstruck '8' measuring 44mm by 28mm was applied in Jersey in 1868 on an unpaid letter to France. In Guernsey a handstruck '8' was applied in 1844–46 on unpaid letters arriving from France.

Handstruck '7' and '8' marks found on letters addressed to France in the 1850s are French marks representing 7 or 8 decimes due.

From 1840 manuscript 1d. and 2d. marks were applied before the handstruck types were introduced and in Jersey one or two manuscript 4d. marks are known during the period of the Uniform Fourpenny Rate from December 5, 1839, to January 9, 1840.

Parcel Post Labels, 1883–1936

Parcel post labels were introduced on August 1, 1883. In *The British Post Office*, C. F. Dendy Marshall listed sixteen different main English types and a number of sub-types. These labels were used in the Channel Islands and a typical example is illustrated in Figure 3.30. Most types show the name of the office, the head office, the telegraphic code address, with special panels in which details of the postage rate, registration, and insurance could be entered, the adhesives stuck, and the datestamp applied. Often the adhesives were cancelled with a different stamp from the datestamp; thus one used at David Place, Jersey, had the David Place c.d.s in the space provided for office stamp and the postage stamps cancelled with the Jersey double-ring rubber parcel post stamp with name across the centre.

They have been recorded for the following places but doubtless others exist:

Jersey: Beaumont, Beresford Street, Cheapside, David Place, First Tower Georgetown, Gorey, Gorey Village, Havre-des-Pas, Jersey, La Rocque, Rouge Bouillon, St. Aubin, St. Brelades Bay, St. Heliers, and Samares.

Guernsey: Catel, Les Gravées, Market Place, Mount Row, St. Andrew's, St. Sampson's, St. Peter-in-the-Wood, Vale Road, Alderney, and Sark.

Only four different types are recorded by the Channel Islands Specialists' Society but others probably exist. The making up of the so-called X Lists, for which these labels were required, ceased in 1914 but stocks in hand after that date were used up. Smaller labels were used in later years but rarely after 1936.

The labels are of interest to specialists because they show examples

3.28(a) Guernsey, 1842–43

3.28(b) Guernsey, 1847

3.29 Jersey, 1851

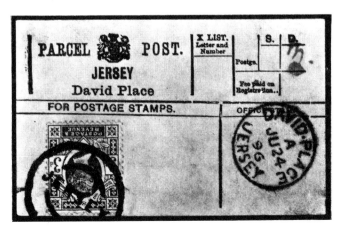

3.30 Parcel post label

of some of the scarcer sub-office datestamps; also because they often bear some denominations of postage stamps not otherwise found on cover.

CUSTOMS DUTY PARCEL POST LABELS

For many years there has been very little duty payable on tobacco in Jersey and Guernsey, where they have their own Customs Services, and a number of London tobacconists used to import parcels of it from the Islands. On November 1, 1895, the British Post Office instituted a service whereby dutiable goods sent from the Channel Islands to Britain could have the charges prepaid by the sender by means of postage stamps. Special green labels with separate spaces for the stamps paying postage and those paying customs duty were brought into use and a handling charge of 1s. per parcel was made. In the early days the labels were used almost entirely for tobacco, but since 1945 other dutiable goods, such as perfume, were sometimes sent and the service was also used for prepayment of purchase tax. The service ceased on September 30, 1969.

The labels measure 89mm wide by 108mm deep ($3\frac{1}{2} \times 4\frac{1}{4}$ in.) and, apart from differences in the size of the lettering, remain much the same today as when they were first brought into use in 1895.

Victorian and Edwardian labels have the stamps paying postage cancelled with a datestamp and those paying duty cancelled with a double-ring rubber stamp normally used as a parcel post cancellation. Later issues have all the stamps cancelled with the same datestamp.

Because in the past most dealers buying the labels have soaked off the stamps, the labels themselves are now quite scarce.

Four types for Guernsey, two for Jersey, and two for Alderney are recorded:

Guernsey: Type 1. 'PARCEL POST' in 3-mm capitals, 'GUERNSEY (GU)' in 2-mm capitals, and the words 'OFFICE STAMP' in the space allotted for the postmark.

Type 2: 'PARCEL POST' in 4-mm capitals, 'GUERNSEY (GU)' in 4-mm and 3-mm upper- and lower-case, and the words 'DATE STAMP' in the space allotted for the postmark.

Type 3: As type 2 but different Arms.

Type 4: As illustrated in Figure 3.31 (lower part).

3.31 Customs duty parcel post labels

Jersey: Type 1. As illustrated in Figure 3.31 (upper part).

Type 2: 'DATE STAMP' instead of 'OFFICE STAMP,' and 'Registration and Express Fees' in two lines in a wider panel instead of 'Fee paid on registration.'

Alderney: Type 1. Name in upper- and lower-case.

Type 2: Names in capitals.

Exact dates of use of the various types are not known but I give the earliest of each seen:

Guernsey: Type 1, 1905; Type 2, 1911; Type 3, 1914; Type 4, 1952.

Jersey: Type 1, 1901; Type 2, 1917.

Alderney: Type 1, 1910; Type 2, 1936; overprinted 'Jersey' by rubber stamp.

FORGED EDWARD VII £1

The frequent use of the £1 Edward for prepayment of customs duty was one of the reasons why a certain London dealer offering forgeries of the stamp for sale in 1913 had them cancelled with a forged Jersey postmark. At the Central Criminal Court, a London stamp dealer was found guilty of selling and having in his possession for sale 2,679 photo-lithographed copies of the Edward VII £1 green and was sentenced to three years penal servitude. The forgeries differed from the genuine stamps in that they were printed on thinner paper with a roughly impressed crown watermark, were slightly deeper in colour, the shading round the head was formed of coloured lines on a white ground, and each had a forged Jersey postmark. They were offered for sale at 8s. each. After the case, most of them were destroyed and the odd copies that occasionally come on the market today readily fetch over £50 apiece, despite their known status.

4

DATESTAMPS
AND OTHER CANCELLATIONS

Jersey

EARLY TYPES

The first datestamp was introduced in Jersey in 1830. It was known as 'the improved steel datestamp with a double set of figures' (Figure 4.1) and is recorded in the Proof Books of the G.P.O. as having been dispatched to Jersey on May 31, 1830. It was taken into use in June, 1830. Towards the end of 1845 the datestamp apparently became too worn for use and was replaced temporily by a 'travelling' or 'skeleton' type made from movable letters in a skeleton frame (Figure 4.2) of which examples have been seen struck in red and dated between October 29 and November 10, 1845. A recut of Figure 4.1 was dispatched from the G.P.O. on November 7, 1845, and was again put into use. An interesting feature of this datestamp is that it appears to have been occasionally used with some figures of the date missing and one example used in 1832 has the date completely missing. This may have been due to carelessness in inserting the figures. Black ink appears to have been used from 1830 to 1843 and red ink from 1843 to 1849. The recut can be distinguished from the original by the letters which are sans-serif.

In 1848 the stamp was again recut and whilst it was away another 'travelling' type was used (Figure 4.3) of which Mr. J. M. Y. Trotter has an example struck in red and dated June 16, 1848. The recut was dispatched to Jersey from the G.P.O. on June 17, 1848. It is known used up to at least April 18, 1849.

4.1

4.2 'Travelling' type, 1845

4.3 'Travelling' type, 1848

35

DOUBLE ARC

4.4

In 1849 the double-arc type was introduced (Figure 4.4). It was dispatched from the G.P.O. in July, 1849, and the earliest date of use seen is October 4, 1849. Three slightly different types are known: (*a*) with J and Y of JERSEY level with the top of date (month); (*b*) with J below top of date and Y level with top; (*c*) with J and Y well above date line. This stamp had a somewhat colourful existence: it started with red in 1849, changed to blue in 1851, then to orange in December, 1852, changed to black in 1854, went to a dirty green in 1855 and to grey-black in mid-1855, reverted to blue in 1857, and ended with black in 1858. Below the date appeared the letters, A, B or C.

NUMERALS

From 1840 to 1880 the Maltese Cross and 409 numeral and duplex types were used to cancel postage stamps, and the other datestamps described above were used chiefly as backstamps. However, examples of Figure 4.1 are known used as cancellations and struck in red or black on the 1841 red-brown. The numeral cancellations are dealt with in Chapter 5.

CIRCULAR DATESTAMPS

4.5

In 1858 a small single-circle datestamp 19mm in diameter was brought into use, chiefly as a backstamp (Figure 4.5). Two examples were dispatched from the G.P.O. on April 22, 1858. They can be found lettered A, B, C, D, E, F, A2, B2, F2, and without any letters at all, and were in use up to the late 1890s. The letters referred to the time of collection and stamps without letters were used for counter work.

Single-circle datestamps ranging from 19 to 25mm in diameter with the name Jersey in short or tall letters round the top and the date in two lines across the centre were in use at various times between 1870 and the 1930s. They are known with the following letters above the date: A, B, C, D, O, and P (telegraphic); also without any letters at all, or with letter and figure combinations such as A1, A2, B1, B2, C1, C2, D1, D2, E1, G2, GFXA, 11XA or with an asterisk. From about 1899 the letters were replaced by the time of the collection or the time the mail was made up.

COMBINED OBLITERATOR

In 1881 what is known as the 'combined obliterator' (Figure 4.6) was introduced to replace the duplex types (*see* Chapter 5). It was dispatched from the G.P.O. on March 15, 1881 and the earliest date of use seen is March 23, 1881. It can be found lettered A, B, C, D, and E and has four corner lines outside the circle. A similar type but with only three corner lines outside the circle was brought into use round about April, 1884, and is known lettered C, D, and E. On December 9, 1886, a slightly larger type, but with two long thin bars forming almost complete circles (except for four breaks of 5mm), one shorter thin bar and solid corners outside the circle, was dispatched from the G.P.O. The earliest date of use seen is September 26, 1887, and the latest November 10, 1896, lettered A, C, D or F. A third type of the smaller obliterator, with one line and a solid corner outside the circle, came into use towards the end of 1892 and appears to have continued until about 1905. It can be found lettered C, D, E, F, G, and H, and from about 1899 with the time instead of a letter. Several of these obliterators appear to have been in use at the same time and the sizes of the letters of JERSEY vary a lot. This obliterator is sometimes known as the 'squared circle'.

4.6

DOUBLE CIRCLES

From 1896 a double-circle datestamp with solid bars separated by a cross was put into service (Figure 4.7). About ten sub-types exist with different sizes of letters and cross and with bars of different thickness. It was used up to 1929. A similar type with a sans-serif figure 1 at the bottom instead of the cross appears to have been introduced in 1906. This can be found in six sub-types with different sizes of letters, figures, and bars. Both types were used concurrently from 1906. Up to 1914 all the Jersey datestamps had the month preceding the day but from then onwards the day preceded the month. (This change was common thoughout Britain.)

4.7

MACHINE CANCELLATIONS

The first machine cancellation was introduced in 1923 (Figure 4.8), followed in 1930 by one having a circular datestamp and continuous

4.8 Datestamp occurs either side of wavy lines and sometimes both sides

wavy lines. It had six bars in 1930–31, five in 1931–35, and seven from 1935 onwards (Figure 4.9). The year 1931 saw the introduction of the first slogan reading 'The Best Investment a Telephone' and this was followed in 1932 by one reading 'The Telephone Makes Life Easier'. This remained in use for about a year and then the continuous wavy lines were reverted to until 1937 when a type with two breaks between the bars was used. The removable centre-piece could be put into the machine either way up. During 1942 continuous lines again appeared but the broken type was again reverted to from 1943. During the Occupation the last two figures were made locally and are easy to recognize. In 1946 the correct figures were again in use and in 1948 the continuous-lines type of 1942 was brought back. Examples used from 1950 show one or two damaged bars and in 1953 the bars with breaks were used again with a new datestamp which lacks the curved line at the bottom. A new stamp with larger letters was introduced in 1960.

Many slogans were used between 1946 and 1969, but these are too numerous to list here. The holiday slogans are still used by the Jersey Postal Administration.

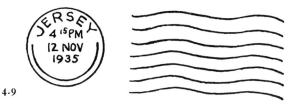

4.9

4.10 Incorrect town name

LATER DATESTAMPS—DOUBLE CIRCLES

About 1930 a double-ring circular datestamp reading JERSEY (ST. HELIERS) CHANNEL ISLANDS was introduced (Figure 4.10). In 1938 a similar type was sent in which the words CHANNEL ISLANDS have been abbreviated to CH. IS.; this is still in use although the correct postal name of the town is St. Helier. The first type has been seen as late as 1944.

A double-circle cancellation reading JERSEY, CHANNEL ISLANDS/1 (serifed), introduced about 1928, was replaced about 1934 by JERSEY/ CHANNEL ISLANDS (Figure 4.11). The year 1945 saw the introduction of a new one reading JERSEY C.I./1 (Figure 4.12) and this has also been seen with a 2 at the bottom. The JERSEY, CHANNEL ISLANDS type was brought back in 1952 with a 3 at the bottom.

4.11

4.12

SINGLE CIRCLES

Several types are in use at present; one introduced in 1935 is shown in Figure 4.13 and reads JERSEY/CHANNEL ISLANDS, the space between the last two words varying.

A type reading JERSEY CHANNEL ISLANDS (Figure 4.14) with numbers 2, 4, 5, 6, 8, 9 or 10 has been in use since 1938 and is to be found with both large and small letters and sometimes with a full stop after JERSEY. One is also known with z above date and a figure 4 below. A datestamp numbered 3 lacks the asterisk over the date and reads JERSEY CHANNEL IS., and there is a similar one without any number. There is also a type in which JERSEY, CHANNEL ISLANDS occupies exactly half the circumference. Large rubber c.d.s. with JERSEY 1 at the top and CH. IS. at the bottom or JERSEY 2 at the top and CHANNEL ISLANDS at the bottom are occasionally met with.

Between 1955 and 1958 single circles with JERSEY CHANNEL ISLANDS were put into use with numbers at the bottom and letters above the date, such as 2 with R above date, 3 with S, 4 with Z, 6 with W, and 7 without letter above the date.

4.13

4.14

THE CROWN REGISTERED MARK

The first registration stamp used in Jersey was the Crown and REGISTERED type (Figure 4.15) which was also used in London and Southampton and in one or two other ports. The P.O. Proof Books record that one was sent to Jersey on December 29, 1858, but as examples are known on covers dated 1855 and 1856 it seems probable that an earlier one was sent. On both the covers referred to the

4.15

4.16

4.17

4.18

4.19

Jersey crown registered mark is applied in black and the London one in red. The postage stamps in each case are cancelled with the 409 numeral.

REGISTRATION CANCELLATIONS

Circular datestamps were usually used for registration purposes on covers and often on parcels, although ovals also exist. The first oval bore only the name of the island (Figure 4.16) and is recorded as being dispatched to Jersey on August 19, 1879. It is known lettered from A to E and without any letter at all. By 1939 (probably earlier) it was replaced by one having JERSEY CHANNEL ISLANDS at the bottom: the letters are small and the words 'Channel Islands' are in upper- and lower-case letters. By 1939 another type with the words JERSEY CHANNEL IS. in small capitals had been introduced (Figure 4.17) but since 1947 another one with larger letters has been in use. Similar stamps in use at present read REGISTERED at the top, JERSEY CHANNEL ISLANDS at the bottom, and have a figure 3 or 4 below the date.

Another type recorded as used on January 29, 1942, and again in December, 1946, bears no date and has the word REGISTERED across the middle (Figure 4.18).

MONEY ORDER OFFICE

The cancellation of the Money Order Office (Figure 4.19) is occasionally seen on parcel post labels and is known cancelling stamps in 1900 (£1), 1904 and 1908 (1d.).

PARCEL POST CANCELLATIONS

The first type of cancellation for parcel post purposes (Figure 4.20) was dispatched from the G.P.O. on November 24, 1886, and was made of rubber. Several examples of its use are known, the latest being on a parcel post label of 1911. The more usual type found is the double-ring rubber type with the name across the middle (Figure 4.21). It was first sent to Jersey on September 9, 1892, others following in 1893, 1894, 1898, and 1904. Several types can be recognized. In one the inner arcs are above and below the first E and in another they come between the J and the E.

The first label type of cancellation was dispatched from the G.P.O. on June 28, 1917, and bore the words PARCEL JE POST/JERSEY/1 and the date all in boxes in the left two-thirds and the letters JE between a pattern of diagonal lines in the right third. A second copy was sent on August 3, 1920.

The last used type is shown in Figure 4.22(*a*) and exists numbered 1, 2 or 3 at the top. Another late type is smaller and includes the name of St. Heliers (Figure 4.22(*b*)). It is struck in mauve.

Several types of rubber cancellation have been used on small packets. They include one of 30mm diameter with JERSEY at the top, CHANNEL ISLANDS at the bottom, and the date and time in two lines across the centre. A figure 1 or 2 appears above the date. There is also a similar one with larger letters and CH. IS. at the bottom, with a figure 1 above the date. A similar type (Figure 4.23) used after the liberation has five bars across the centre instead of any date. Figure 4.24 without ST. HELIERS was dispatched to Jersey on October 9, 1893. One with (ST. HELIERS) was sent on March 7, 1898, and further examples on September 23, 1905, and June 24, 1909. A larger type, 42mm in diameter, is known cancelling a 1951 K.G. VI 2d. pale red-brown on a newspaper wrapper addressed to Southampton. A roller type as below was used on small packets in 1957 but it wore out in a few weeks.

4.20

4.21

Another small rectangular cancel reading JERSEY (ST. HELIERS)/ CHANNEL ISLANDS with the date across the centre is known used in 1938.

(a)

4.22

(b)

4.23   4.24

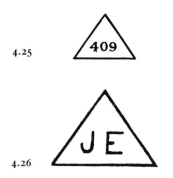

4.25

4.26

TRIANGLES

Triangular cancellations are used on circulars printed in imitation
typewritten characters and bear the figures or telegraphic code letters
allotted to the post office by the G.P.O. A small 409 in triangle
(Figure 4.25) is known on King Edward VII ½d. stamps and on the
Occupation issue; it was dispatched on August 4, 1909. A larger
triangle with the letters JE is known on a wartime cover and is possibly still in use (Figure 4.26). There is also a larger 409 in triangle
used as part of a machine cancellation in conjunction with the wavy
lines. Two types exist. These were used recently on a count of letters.

'PAID' STAMPS

From the 1920s various PAID handstamps, applied in red, are to be
found, usually on news-wrappers or circulars. A type with movable
letters and another with fixed ½d. were sent from the G.P.O. on
June 26, 1919. The 2½d. value (Figure 4.27) was used during the
German Occupation when postage stamps were not available, when
the franking machine was being repaired, or when supplies of
electricity were cut off. A failure of paper supplies in 1942 prevented
any stamps being printed for some months and this cancellation had
to be put into use. It can also be found on mail posted after November 15, 1944, when stamp supplies finally ran out. Some envelopes
with this stamp without date were sold in quantities of a dozen and
over to residents of country districts and were posted in pillar boxes.

42

On arrival at the Head Post Office they were cancelled with the normal machine cancellation. This avoided a journey into St. Helier for letters to be franked when stamps were unobtainable.

A PAID 1d. handstamp was also used in 1941 before the first Jersey 1d. stamp was ready, and again later on. Another 1d. value appears to have been made by removing the 2 from the $\frac{1}{2}$d., but no examples of the original $\frac{1}{2}$d. used properly are known to me. When the printed paper rate was raised to 1$\frac{1}{2}$d. in 1952 a new PAID stamp for this value, similar to the 2$\frac{1}{2}$d. one, was issued. Higher values were introduced as postal rates increased up to 1969.

4.27

MACHINE 'PAID' STAMPS

Information on the earlier types of machine PAID cancellations is very scant but the first type is believed to have consisted of the words JERSEY/PAID $\frac{1}{2}$d./date in three lines and used from about 1926 to 1929. In the latter year the words GREAT BRITAIN were added. This was used in conjunction with the bars of the first cancelling machine. There followed in 1932 a boxed type with an inner square in which appeared $\frac{1}{2}$D and the date in two lines below; in the outer square appeared the inscription JERSEY/PAID (top and bottom) and GREAT BRITAIN (left and right, both reading upwards). This was followed about 1937 by a type having $\frac{1}{2}$D/PAID in two lines between two sets of seven wavy lines, with a circular datestamp inscribed JERSEY/GT. BRITAIN and having the date in two lines across the centre. A similar die with 1D/PAID was introduced when postage was raised in 1940 and was used when adhesives ran out at various times during the Occupation. When the printed paper rate was raised to 1$\frac{1}{2}$d. in 1952 a 1$\frac{1}{2}$d. die was brought into use. Higher values were introduced as postal rates increased up to 1969. All the PAID stamps were struck in red.

METER STAMP

During the Occupation a meter stamp, Neopost No. 8, was used at the head office, St. Helier, at first as a $\frac{1}{2}$d. stamp with the die cracked vertically; the die seems to have been repaired and later it was often used as a 2$\frac{1}{2}$d. stamp.

43

Guernsey

EARLY TYPES

The first Guernsey datestamp also went into use in 1830 and was similar to Figure 4.1 of Jersey. It is recorded in the P.O. Proof Books as having been dispatched on May 31, 1830, and it was in use in June. The datestamp was recut in 1843. The letter N appears to have been repaired and a new set of figures supplied. The 4's are sans-serif. This stamp was dispatched from the G.P.O., London, on July 29, 1843. Mr. J. M. Y. Trotter has a 'skeleton' type used on July 28, 1843. Throughout 1844 when a 4 occurred in the day of the month an inverted 7 was used for the first 4 of 1844. It is thought possible that in 1833 the postmaster postmarked the letters either a day earlier or a day later when a 3 occurred in the day of the month. In 1847 this stamp gave out and was replaced from the end of July until mid-August with a 'travelling' or 'skeleton' type (Figure 4.28) of which dates between July 29 and August 13 have been recorded.

4.28

DOUBLE ARC

In 1847 the double-arc type (similar to Jersey Figure 4.4) lettered A, B or C was introduced. It was dispatched from the G.P.O. on August 15 and the earliest date of use is August 18. Three slightly different types can be recorded: (*a*) with G of GUERNSEY below bottom of date line, Y above date line and arcs less than 3mm apart; (*b*) with G and Y well below bottom of date line (the Y actually points to the bottom of year line) and arcs 3mm apart; (*c*) with G and Y well above bottom of date line and arcs 3mm apart. Between 1847 and mid-1858 when it went out of use the datestamp was struck in a variety of colours. It started with black in 1847, changed to blue in 1849, then to various shades of yellow (usually rather a mustard colour) from January 1853, reverted to black via a rust colour in 1854, went to a dirty green in 1856, and ended in blue-black in 1858. Type (*a*) appears to have been used from 1847 to 1852, type (*b*) from 1852 to 1858, and type (*c*) from late October 1853 to mid-1858. The two latter types are recorded as being dispatched from the G.P.O. on December 27, 1851, and October 14, 1853, respectively.

NUMERALS

From 1840 to 1886 the Maltese Cross and 324 numeral and duplex types were used to cancel postage stamps and the datestamps were used as backstamps.

CIRCULAR DATESTAMPS

A small circular datestamp 19mm in diameter was introduced in 1858. An example is recorded in the Proof Books as having been dispatched on January 29, 1858. It was used as a backstamp on letters arriving in the island and is found lettered A, B or C. Three slightly different types were used between 1858 and 1872.

Other single-circle datestamps ranging from 19 to 25mm in diameter with the name GUERNSEY in small or large letters round the top and the date in two lines across the centre were used between 1870 and the 1930s. They are known with the following letters above the date: A, B, C, and D; also with an asterisk or without any letters at all. From 1899 the letters were replaced by the actual time of the collection.

COMBINED OBLITERATOR

The 'combined obliterator' (similar to Jersey Figure 4.6 but larger) was introduced in 1887 and the earliest example that I know is dated December, 1887. It started with four corner lines outside the circle and was lettered A, B, C or D. In 1896 the letters were replaced by the time of posting and in 1902 a slightly smaller type having three corner lines was taken into use (it may have been a recut of the original) and continued until 1905.

DOUBLE CIRCLES

A double-circle datestamp with solid bars separated by a cross was put into service in 1905 and the earliest date recorded is March 24. There are several sub-types with different sizes of letters and cross, and with bars of different thickness. This stamp remained in use up to 1929. Up to 1914 all Guernsey datestamps had the month preceding the day but from then onwards the day preceded the month.

4.29

MACHINE CANCELLATIONS

In June, 1923, the first machine cancellation was introduced. It consisted of five wavy bars and two square datestamps (as Jersey Figure 4.8) and remained in use until December, 1931, when it was succeeded by a type with five wavy bars and a circular datestamp (Figure 4.29). This was replaced in 1936 by a seven-bar type with two breaks between the bars, which in its turn was replaced with another seven-bar type with continuous lines which was used throughout the German Occupation. In 1941 the figure 0 was split to make the final 1 of the year and up to 1945 the last two figures were made locally. In May, 1945, the seven bars with breaks were used again with a new datestamp without the inner bar at the bottom. The continuous bars came back again in mid-1947 but in May, 1948, the bars with breaks were used again with a new datestamp with tall thin letters occupying half the circle and a semi-circular bar which almost touched the G and Y of GUERNSEY. This datestamp cracked in November, and in February, 1949, the old original datestamp of 1932 was brought back into service. It was replaced in January, 1955, with a new datestamp. The bars of all the above types were removable and reversible and could be used with any of the datestamps. Those with the breaks were made so that the centre-piece could be removed for insertion of the PAID dies for use on bulk-posted correspondence.

New datestamps were introduced from time to time between 1957 and 1969.

A large variety of slogans was used between 1947 and 1969. They are too numerous to list in detail.

LATER DATESTAMPS—DOUBLE CIRCLES

In 1929 a double-ring circular datestamp worded GUERNSEY (ST.

PETER PORT) CHANNEL IS. was introduced. The earliest recorded date of use is December 20. It was replaced in 1937 by a similar type in which CHANNEL IS. has been abbreviated to CH. IS. (Figure 4.30), in use until September 30, 1969.

Other double-circle types seen are GUERNSEY C.I./1 and GUERNSEY C.I./2 with black bars between the town name and the number. All examples are postwar and it is believed that they were introduced in 1945 for use in case the cancelling machine broke down.

4.30

SINGLE CIRCLES

A number of new single-circle types, introduced in the late 1930s, were in use until September 30, 1969. They are mostly 23–24mm in diameter and all have GUERNSEY at the top and CHANNEL ISLANDS at the bottom (Figure 4.31). One example has a full stop between CHANNEL . ISLANDS; another reads GUERNSEY CHANNEL ISLANDS round the circumference (Figure 4.32), and a similar one has a figure 1 at the bottom. A rare type used as a cancelling stamp in 1945 and 1946 for very short periods had GUERNSEY CH. IS. at the top and PARCEL DEPOT at the bottom. It was probably meant for post office dockets. During the Occupation these stamps were used with the last two figures of the date made locally (Figure 4.33). In 1948 the same series of single circles had numbers from 5 to 11 inserted above the date and was used on registered mail and postal orders. Another with figure 12 reads GUERNSEY (ST. PETER PORT) CHAN. IS. and was taken into use in 1952. It was used mainly at rush times like Christmas. In August 1954 the figures were replaced by letters running from E to M (except I).

4.31

4.32

1942   1943   1944   4.33

COMMEMORATIVE CANCELLATION

The only commemorative cancellation used under the British postal administration was the 1810 scroll in a rectangular frame inscribed 'POSTAL HISTORY SOCIETY/23rd ANNUAL CONFERENCE/21 OCTOBER 1967/GUERNSEY' (Figure 4.34).

4·34

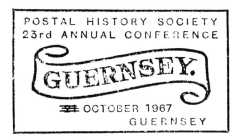

CROWN REGISTERED MARK

A Crown Registered mark is known used in 1852. It is rather similar to Figure 4.15 of Jersey and is struck in blue. It is extremely rare.

REGISTRATION CANCELLATIONS

The earliest oval registered cancellations recorded for Guernsey are one of about 40 × 28mm used to cancel stamps in 1938 and another, 40 × 28mm, on the back of a letter dated 1940. A rubber stamp was made locally during the Occupation. A type issued in 1945 measures about 38 × 25mm and reads GUERNSEY at the top, CHANNEL ISLANDS at the bottom, and REGISTERED across the centre (as Figure 4.18). A more recent one, made of rubber, reads REGISTERED at the top, GUERNSEY CH. IS at the bottom, and has the date across the centre in a single line. This has been seen in mauve on a pair of the 1d. Liberation dated June 25, 1948. It measures 38 × 28mm.

MONEY ORDER OFFICE

A datestamp reading GUERNSEY at the top and M.O.O. at the bottom is known cancelling stamps at various dates between 1886 and 1913 (as Jersey Figure 4.19).

4·35

PARCEL POST CANCELLATIONS

The first parcel post cancellation (Figure 4.35) was made of rubber. It was issued in 1886 and remained in use for about three years until superseded in the autumn of 1889 by the more familiar double-ring rubber type with name across the centre (Figure 4.36). Of this latter type no less than seventeen examples were sent between 1889 and 1905. One had serifed letters, all the other sans-serif. Several sub-types can be identified and there are: (*a*) tall thin letters $4\frac{1}{2}$mm high with arcs of inner circle over the left-hand side of the final E; (*b*) thicker letters 4mm high with arcs over right-hand side of E; (*c*) letters 3mm high with arcs as in (*b*) but farther away from letter. About 1910 a similar stamp reading GUERNSEY/ST. PETER PORT in two lines was introduced; both types were in use together until 1915 when the first label type of cancellation was put into service (Figure 4.37). It was superseded in 1925 by a slightly different type with GUERNSEY/ CHANNEL ISLANDS occupying the upper part of the left two-thirds and PARCEL POST across the centre of the right-hand third in place of the GU.

Another type was Figure 4.38. There was also a smaller type rather

4.36

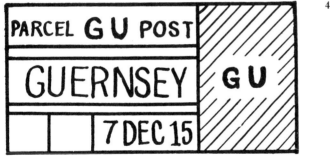

4.37

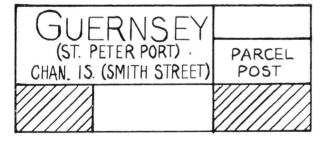

4.38

49

similar to Figure 4.23 but worded GUERNSEY/CHANNEL ISLANDS in two lines across the centre.

In 1956 a new parcel post cancellation was put into use. It is of the same shape and size as Figure 4.37 but is laid out rather differently. In three of the corners (top and bottom left and bottom right) is a cross-hatched shading. At the left and right are panels with PARCEL reading upwards at the left and POST reading upwards at the right. The centre is divided into three panels. SMITH STREET is in the top one, the date in the centre and GUERNSEY (ST. PETER PORT) CHAN. IS. in the bottom panel. This one was soon withdrawn, probably because Smith Street was put in the top by error, and was replaced by one with GUERNSEY in the top and (ST. PETER PORT) CHAN: IS. (SMITH ST.) in the bottom.

There have been many rubber stamps in use, all short-lived, with various inscriptions. It is impossible to list them all but those seen include a circular stamp 30mm in diameter reading GUERNSEY at the top and CHANNEL ISLANDS at the bottom with the date (and sometimes the time) across the centre; a similar circle with GUERNSEY ST. PETER PORT round the top and CHANNEL IS. round the bottom; a small rectangle 50 × 20mm with GUERNSEY/date/CHANNEL ISLANDS in three lines, and a roller type reading thus:

GUERNSEY	GUERNSEY
(ST. PETER PORT)	(ST. PETER PORT)
CHAN. ISLES (SMITH ST)	CHAN. ISLES (SMITH ST)

TRIANGLES

4.39

Two types of triangular cancellation are known for use on bulk postings of circulars in imitation typewritten characters: GU in large triangle (Figure 4.39); 324 in smaller triangle used in the cancelling machine.

'PAID' STAMPS

Two PAID handstamps were sent to Guernsey on August 10, 1920. One had movable figures and the other had a fixed ½d. They were always struck in red and were used up to 1940 when the ½d. was dropped and a 2½d. was introduced to meet the increased letter rate. During the Occupation 1d. and 2½d. stamps were used with locally made year figures which fitted rather badly and did not always show. They are reported to have been used in January, October, and November, 1943, and from April, 1945, on letters prepaid in cash at the head office owing to shortages of adhesive stamps, but were used at other times on bulk postings in the normal way.

When the printed paper rate was raised to 1½d. in 1952 new movable figures for this value were introduced. Higher values were put into as postal rates increased up to 1969.

An example of the 2½d. is known as a cancellation on a 2½d. Occupation stamp; a most unusual usage.

MACHINE 'PAID' STAMPS

The first machine PAID stamp was introduced in 1926. It consisted of the words GUERNSEY/PAID ½D/date in three lines to the left of a set of five wavy lines. It was a roller type and parts of two impressions are usually found on each entire. In 1929 the words GREAT BRITAIN were added to the inscription. From 1932 there was a boxed type with an inner square in which appeared ½D and the date in two lines below,

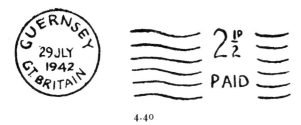

4.40

whilst the outer square contained GUERNSEY/PAID (top and bottom) and GREAT/BRITAIN (left and right, both reading upwards). This was followed in 1936 by a type having ½D/PAID in two lines between two sets of seven wavy lines, and a circular datestamp inscribed GUERNSEY/ GT. BRITAIN with the date in two lines across the centre (Figure 4.40). New 1d. and 2½d. dies were put into use when postage was raised on May 1, 1940, and a 1½d. die in 1952. Others were added as rates increased up to 1969.

During the Occupation locally made year figures were used.

In some cases the ordinary datestamp with inner bar at the bottom instead of GREAT BRITAIN was used in conjunction with the PAID dies because the operator could not be bothered to change it. The PAID dies are, of course, used in the same cancelling machines that are used for ordinary mail, but are struck in red.

5

THE NUMERAL OBLITERATIONS
AND INSTRUCTIONAL MARKS

When the numeral obliterations were allotted throughout the
British Isles in 1844, Guernsey and Jersey were given numbers in the
England and Wales series. Guernsey received the number 324 and
Jersey 409, and obliterators were dispatched from the G.P.O. in
April, 1844. The number 965 was allocated to Alderney in 1848 and
an obliterator was dispatched on May 4.

JERSEY

Eleven different types were in use in Jersey between 1844 and 1902.
The first (Figure 5.1) was that sent out in April, 1844, which had the
number 409 with two curved bars on each side of it and three bars
above and below, the whole making an oval of which the curved
bars form the sides.

5.1   Type 1

The second type was a recut of the first and came into use in July,
1857 (Figure 5.2). It can be distinguished by its figures, which are
much smaller ($5\frac{1}{2}$mm high against 7mm of the original figures). The
loop of the 4 is 4mm wide and the cross bar just under 2mm from the
base. There is also a similar type with a blunt point to the 4.

Type 3 is very similar to the first type, but the cross bar of the 4 is
2mm from the base, the loop of the 4 is 3mm wide and the height of
the figures is $6\frac{1}{2}$mm. The type 1 obliterator is $22\frac{1}{2}$mm wide and the
type 3 $21\frac{1}{2}$mm. Type 3 appears to have been used from 1861 to 1864
and is mainly found on letters addressed to the Continent and on
French stamps used on the Boîte Mobile Service.

5.2   Type 2

Type 4 is again somewhat similar to type 1, but the cross bar of the
4 is 3mm from the base. It appears to have been used from 1864 to

5.3 Type 5

5.4 Type 6

5.5 Type 7

5.6 Type 8

1870 and is often heavily struck so that the horizontal and vertical bars appear to form an unbroken oval. It is known on a number of letters addressed to France and on French stamps from the Boîte Mobile Service, but was not used exclusively for this purpose.

The fifth type (Figure 5.3) is the first of the duplexes. It was dispatched from the G.P.O. on April 22, 1858, and the earliest date of use recorded is October 14, 1858. It was replaced about 1863 by a very similar one having a datestamp 19mm wide (1mm wider than the one it replaced).

The sixth type had the numeral part of the duplex changed from horizontal to vertical format (Figure 5.4). The oval is 20–21mm in diameter and the loop of the 9 is oval. It was sent to Jersey on October 15, 1866, and the earliest date that I have seen it used is November 4.

Type 7 (shown as Figure 5.5) is the largest of all the duplexes. The oval is 22–23mm in diameter and the loop of the 9 is rounder. It was dispatched from the G.P.O. on January 17, 1870, and the earliest date of use recorded is February 25. It remained in use until 1874.

The last of the duplex types (Figure 5.6) was taken into use in 1872 and remained in use until 1880. The earliest date seen is November 14, 1872, and the latest August 27, 1880. The datestamp has the name JERSEY around the circumference. There are two slightly different types of this stamp: (a) is 19mm in diameter and has a sharp point to the 4 (Figure 5.7); (b) is 18mm in diameter and has a blunt point to the 4 (Figure 5.8).

What appears to be a sub-type of type 8 is dated February 5, 1881, and is lettered A in the datestamp. The numerals are shorter, the zero is rounder, and the upright of the 4 leans over to the right. The lettering in the datestamp is also larger.

Types 5, 6 and 7 are lettered A, B or C (an example of type 7 is also known lettered O in 1874), and type 8 is lettered B, C or D in the datestamp.

Type 9 is a single obliterator used mainly on newspapers and on mail arriving from France on the Boîte Mobile Service between 1875 and 1881. It is 19mm wide and has three bars at the top and bottom. The early type (Figure 5.9) has a full stop after the 9 and the tip of the 4 is 2mm from the upright. A later type, found on the Peace and Commerce issues, has no stop after the 9, the tip of the 4 is 3mm from the upright, and the 0 and 9 almost touch each other (Figure 5.10).

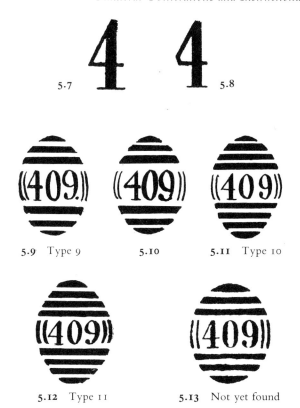

5.7   **5.8**

5.9   Type 9   **5.10**   **5.11**   Type 10

5.12   Type 11   **5.13**   Not yet found

Type 10 is almost a single obliterator 19–20mm in diameter. It was used almost exclusively on registered mail and is known used in conjunction with the oval registered stamp between 1888 and 1902 (Figure 5.11).

Type 11 is known on a 1d. red plate 149. It is 20mm in diameter (Figure 5.12).

There is also a further type that should be mentioned although no examples of it have yet been seen. On November 16, 1881, the G.P.O. dispatched to Jersey a large oval obliterator (Figure 5.13) and a separate datestamp. It was marked 'For Stamping Machine 180504'.

There are several single obliterators rather similar to Figures 5.9 to 5.12 but differing slightly in detail.

5.14 Type 1

5.15 Type 2

5.16 Type 3

Eight types of numeral obliterator can be recorded for Guernsey between 1844 and 1888. The first was sent out in April, 1844, and was put into use in May (Figure 5.14).

Type 2 is described in the Proof Books as a recut of the original and was dispatched from the G.P.O. on October 14, 1853 (Figure 5.15). The earliest date seen is February 15, 1854. It can be distinguished from the original by the figures, which are considerably smaller (5mm high against the 6½mm of type 1).

Type 3 is very similar to type 1, but has the serif of the 2 pointing to the point of the 4 instead of being almost vertical (Figure 5.16). It is known used in 1857. There is also a similar type with the bottom loop of the 3 much flatter.

Type 4 is the first duplex (Figure 5.17). It was dispatched from the G.P.O. on June 15, 1858, and can be identified when off cover because it has a much rounder appearance than the single obliterator. The earliest date of use seen is September 6, 1858.

In July, 1860, two further examples of a duplex similar to type 4, but having a datestamp closer to the numeral and with the figures of date more widely spaced, were dispatched from the G.P.O. (Figure 5.18). In the numeral part of this obliterator the centre point of the 3 is straight instead of pointing downwards as in the previous type, the serif of the 2 is well clear of the curve of the 2, the foot of the 2 and loop of the 4 are larger, and the 4 has a flat top. The earliest date of use recorded is January 23, 1861. Types 4 and 5 were both in use until the autumn of 1867.

By November 14, 1867, a new type with vertical oval containing the numerals 324 was introduced (Figure 5.19). It remained in use until replaced by a similar but heavier type in 1875 (Figure 5.20). These

5.17 Type 4

5.18 Type 5

two types are very difficult to distinguish off cover, but type 6 has a larger datestamp with larger letters than type 7. The numeral parts differ in the following ways: type 6 has a short foot to the 2 and the serif points to the point of the 4; type 7 has a longer foot to the 2 and the serif points inside the 4. The bars of type 7 are heavier than type 6, and there is very little space between the bottom two.

Type 8 was put into use in 1880, and the earliest date recorded is February 28. It is a much lighter type than the previous two, and the figure 4 is much narrower. It is known used up to 1888 (Figure 5.21). An example used in 1887 appears to be much heavier and has the centre point of the 3 horizontal instead of sloping downwards, the serif of the 2 almost vertical, and the top of the 4 more pointed. This is possibly due to wear, or else the stamp needed cleaning.

Two vertical 324 single obliterators are known used on newspapers. A type with three bars at top and bottom was used in 1874 and one with two bars at top and bottom in 1890. There was also a three-bar type with flat-topped 3.

ALDERNEY

The Alderney numeral 965 was allotted in May, 1848. A superb example of it on an 1841 1d. red-brown is shown in Figure 5.22. This type has been seen used from 1848 to the mid-1860s, and a different type, with three bars top and bottom, slightly narrower figures, a thicker top bar to the 5, and measuring 22mm across, from the mid-1860s to 1895 (Figure 5.23). Both types are known on the 1d. lilac.

Figure 5.24 appears to be a vertical type of 965, but no such type was in use in Alderney. A postcard has now been found with the

5.19   Type 6

5.20   Type 7

5.21   Type 8

5.22   5.23   5.24

5.25

5.26

**POSTED OUT
OF COURSE**

5.27

5.28

Gone Away
409

5.29

Liable to Letter Rate
409

5.30

vertical 965 forming part of a duplex with the Winchfield datestamp of July 15, 1897. It would appear that in 1897 a new duplex stamp was sent to Winchfield with the number 965 instead of the correct number 963. Any vertical 965 cancellation must therefore be part of the Winchfield error.

Instructional Marks

The instructional markings fall into three groups: (*a*) those with a figure showing the amount due; (*b*) those explaining the reason for the charge; (*c*) those explaining some irregularity in transmission which does not involve an extra charge. Many of these marks are or were issued throughout the British Isles and can only be allocated to a particular office if the cover possesses other identifying marks. These are, in the main, excluded from this account. Most marks, however, include the number allotted in 1844. The usual procedure was for the office of dispatch to impress on underpaid letters a mark in red indicating the charge to be collected and the reason for it. If an underpayment was first noticed at the office of arrival the mark should have been applied in black. Jersey (409) usually did this correctly, but Guernsey (324) nearly always used black ink only. Marks in group (*c*) were usually impressed in purple, latterly sometimes in green.

JERSEY

The earliest charge marks recorded in the G.P.O. Proof Books (December, 1880) are for ½d. and 1d. of a type common to many provincial towns. They bore no identifying numbers. The next one takes the form of a large 2 with 409 below it in an oval frame (Figure 5.25). It was dispatched in February, 1883, but the only example seen is on an unpaid letter to London dated March, 2, 1896.

The earliest mark of any kind recorded (December, 1879) is from group (*b*) and reads 'Contains a communication/of the nature of a Letter/409' in three lines. This was followed in November, 1880, by similar ones reading 'Contrary to regulations/409', 'Prohibited enclosure/409' and 'Closed contrary/to regulations/409'. They cover a breach of regulations that anything sent at a lower rate than that for letters must be left open at the ends and not contain any enclosure.

In February, 1882, appeared 'More to pay/above—oz/409' (Figure 5.26). Presumably all these marks are still valid for use, but none has been seen. Those of this kind in current use include 'Posted out/of course' (Figure 5.27), 'Not Known/409' (Figure 5.28), 'Gone Away/409' (Figure 5.29), 'Liable to Letter Rate/409' (Figure 5.30)—this is known on postcards from France (in 1903–05) that were intended for internal use only.

Postcards of 1904–06 are known bearing the 1d. mark shown as Figure 5.31, but this was later replaced by Figure 5.32. The addition of the words 'To Pay' was made in Great Britain about 1918, but some of the older marks still persist. Others in recent use are shown in Figures 5.33 to 5.35. The 3d. was sent in 1914 and the 4d., with a 5d. of the same type, in 1921.

The mark most commonly met with on unstamped letters was Figure 5.36. If the amount due was 5d. this was usually stamped in red in a second operation, but other values were written in. This mark seems to have been used for any charge above 4d., even if some stamps were affixed. Deficient postage on letters may also be indicated by Figure 5.37. One that found a fair amount of use when the rate for postcards bearing a conventional message went up from 1d. to 1½d. is shown as Figure 5.38.

Other marks known are: 'Closed contrary/to regulations/409', as Figure 5.30; '1½d./TO PAY/409', as Figure 5.32 (known dated 1924); '2½d./TO PAY/409' (1957); '3½d./TO PAY/409' (1957), as Figure 5.35; 'TO PAY/POSTED/OUT OF/COURSE', as Figure 5.36; '1d./TO PAY/LIABLE TO/LETTER RATE/409', as Figure 5.38; 'More to pay/Letter Rate above . . . oz.,' as Figure 5.37 (1957); 'TO PAY/CONTRARY TO/REGULATIONS/LIABLE TO/ . . . RATE', as Figure 5.37; 'MISSENT TO JERSEY', 5 × 32mm,

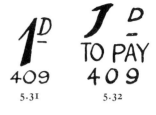

5.31   5.32

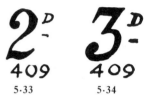

5.33   5.34

5.35

5.36

5.37

5.38

in mauve on letter dated 1958; large box type headed 'RETURN TO SENDER/UNDELIVERED FOR REASON STATED', with the following in two columns with a space for a tick by each: 'Gone away, Not Known, Not Occupied, No Such Address in, Deceased, Refused, Not Called For, Insufficiently Addressed', with 409 at the bottom; used in 1959.

A hexagonal mark with large T with figure below it (5 and 15 seen) and JE below the frame was used around the turn of the century on postcards and letters passing between Jersey and France. The 20, 30, 40, and 50 were sent on September 28, 1907. The T denoted Taxe and the amount was recorded in gold centimes (5c. = $\frac{1}{2}$d.) as required by the U.P.U. Some of the 5c. cards also bear the 1d./409 mark to denote how much was to be collected in Jersey.

GUERNSEY

5.39

The Guernsey marks seen include Figures 5.29, 5.30, 5.36 (in black and purple), and 5.38. The hexagonal T mark for Guernsey (GU) (Figure 5.39) is known on a postcard addressed to France in 1893, denoting 15c. underpaid. Double this amount was collected at Caen and the postage-due stamp affixed.

The modern postage-due marks are shown in Figures 5.40 to 5.44. Figure 5.45 was struck in purple on returned printed matter and a somewhat similar 1d. one with 'Undelivered for/reason stated' in upper- and lower-case and 324 omitted was used before and during the German Occupation. Figure 5.46 is a type introduced towards the end of 1956.

Others seen are: 'Found in course/of sorting', as Figure 5.27; '1D./TO PAY/ LIABLE TO/LETTER RATE/324', as Figure 5.38; '6D./TO PAY/ POSTED UNPAID/324' and '8D./TO PAY/POSTED UNPAID/324' as Figure 5.36'; also similar type with value tablet blank; 'More to pay/above

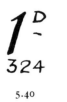

5.40

5.41

5.42

5.43

5.44

```
┌─────────────────────────────┐   ┌───────────────────────────────┐
│ UNDELIVERED FOR             │   │ GUERNSEY            │ INITIALS  │
│ REASON STATED               │   │ CHANNEL  ISLANDS    │           │
├─────────────────────────────┤   ├─────────────────────┤           │
│  D   │                      │   │ GONE  AWAY          │           │
│  1 1 │ POSTAGE DUE          │   │ ADDRESS UNKNOWN     │           │
│  ─ ─ │ FOR RETURN           │   │ ROAD  UNKNOWN       │           │
│  1 2 │       TO             │   │ NAME  UNKNOWN       │           │
│  ─   │    SENDER            │   │ INSUFFICIENT        │           │
│ 324  │                      │   │         ADDRESS     │           │
│      │                      │   │ NO POST TOWN        │           │
│      │                      │   │ ADDRESSEE           │           │
│      │                      │   │       DECEASED      │           │
└──────┴──────────────────────┘   └─────────────────────┴───────────┘
```

5.45   5.46

. . . oz/324', as Figure 5.26; 'D./MORE TO/PAY/LETTER RATE/above . . . oz.', as Figure 5.37; 'More to pay/Letter rate above . . . oz.' as Figure 5.44; similar stamp to Figure 5.45 but with 2d. instead of 1½d.; Figure 5.39 also exists with the following figures – 5, 10, 20, and 40; 'TO PAY/POSTAGE CANNOT BE/PREPAID BY MEANS/OF AN INCOMPLETE/FRANKING IMPRESSION/LIABLE TO . . . RATE/324'; large box type headed 'RETURN TO SENDER/UNDELIVERED FOR REASON STATED', with the following in smaller capitals below in two columns with space for tick by the side of each: 'GONE AWAY, NOT KNOWN, NOT OCCUPIED, NO SUCH ADDRESS IN, NO POST TOWN, DECEASED, REFUSED, NOT CALLED FOR, INSUFFICIENTLY ADDRESSED', with 324 at the bottom; 'SURCHARGE DUE/TO INCREASED/POSTAL CHARGES/324'. A boxed 'MISSENT TO GUERNSEY' in violet has been in use since 1954.

Alderney and Sark are sub-offices of Guernsey and have no instructional marks of their own. The number 965 formerly allotted to Alderney is now used at Heywood, Lancs.

MANUSCRIPT MARKS

A number of early letters from Jersey and Guernsey have manuscript endorsements and the following are recorded: 'Missent to (Jersey datestamp of 1848)'; 'Not found' in red on a Jersey letter of 1842; 'Not known' in red on a letter from the Isle of Wight to Guernsey in 1857; 'Now residing in London/Address not known' in red on a letter from Newark to Guernsey in 1841; 'Left for St. Malow from (Guernsey datestamp of 1855)'; 'More to pay' and large figure 2 in black on letter from Guernsey to Jersey of 1856.

6

LOCAL DELIVERY SERVICES

Guernsey Electric Railway

6.1

Towards the end of the nineteenth century a number of British tramway companies issued stamps for prepayment of parcels carried by their services.

In 1905 the Guernsey Electric Railway Company issued a large 1d. brown on green stamp, perforated 11 at sides and imperforate at the top and bottom (Figure 6.1). It is inscribed 'Parcel Ticket' and has a serial number in black at the bottom. For how long the stamp was used is not known but it is now very rare. It is illustrated and recorded in *Morley's Philatelic Journal* of November, 1905, and is believed to have been issued in the autumn of that year.

There was also a 2d. brown on orange in the same design but it has not yet been possible to find out when it was issued.

Four other typeset stamps are also known for this company and they are believed to have been issued before those described above.

The first two are somewhat similar to the above design but have the value in a diamond in the centre with 'GUERNSEY ELECTRIC RAILWAY COMPANY' set out in a diamond pattern with one word along each side (Figure 6.2) Values are 1d. black on pink, 1d. black on white, and 2d. black on blue; perf. 11 at top, imperf. on the other three sides. Their date of issue is believed to be somewhere around 1893.

The other two have the type set in the form of a square within double lines of type with blunt corners (Figure 6.3). At the top is 'Guernsey Railway,' at the bottom 'Company, Ltd.,' at the left 'Parcel,' and at the right 'Ticket.' The value, 2d., appears in the centre. On one stamp it is printed in green on yellow-buff and on the other in black on yellow. The stamps are perforated 11 at the top or on one side and imperf. on the other three sides. They were issued somewhere between 1879 and 1892.

All these stamps were evidently printed in rolls and not in sheets.

The Guernsey Steam Tramway was opened on May 6, 1879. It ran due north from St. Peter Port to St. Sampson's Harbour $2\frac{1}{4}$ miles away, and had six locomotives. There was a single-line track of 4ft $8\frac{1}{2}$in. gauge with a loop at Salette Battery half-a-mile from St. Peter Port, and stations at Vale Road and Channel Islands Road.

The tramway was electrified with an overhead wire in 1892 and then became the Guernsey Electric Railway. It then had eleven motor coaches (double deck) and eight trailers (six open, one closed, and one double deck). The tramway was closed on June 9, 1934, when the company introduced motor buses.

In October, 1907, the Guernsey Post Office concluded an agreement with the Guernsey Railway Company whereby mails were conveyed by tram from St. Sampson's to St. Peter Port. The bags were padlocked in the driver's compartment by the Sub-Postmaster of St. Sampson's and the tram was met at St. Peter Port by a postman who held a key of the padlock. He conveyed the mail from the terminus to the Head Post Office on foot.

The same company also conveyed mails by omnibus from The Vale, Vale Road, and L'Islet from the same date in 1907. The bags were secured in similar fashion as on the trams, near the driver, by the respective Sub-Postmasters. These services continued until June, 1934, when the trams were withdrawn from service. The mail was then conveyed from St. Sampson's to St. Peter Port by omnibus and all the services continued until the Post Office provided its own transport in 1935.

The Jersey Railways

Two light railways functioned in Jersey: the Jersey Railway (later known as the Jersey Western Railway) and the Jersey Eastern Railway. A map is given in Figure 6.4.

The Jersey Railway opened on September 28, 1870, with a standard gauge line from St. Helier to St. Aubin. It was extended to La

6.2

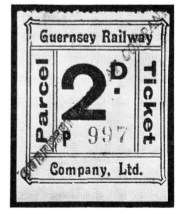

6.3

63

C*

Moye and the existing section was relaid to 3ft 6in. gauge on August 5, 1885. It was extended to Corbière in 1899. The main terminus was at the Weighbridge, St. Helier, and there were stations at West Park, First Tower, Millbrook, Bel Royal, Beaumont, La Haule, St. Aubin, Greenville, Pont Marquet, Don Bridge, Blanches Banques, La Moye, and Corbière. Because of a fire on October 19, 1936, the railway closed and did not reopen.

The Jersey Eastern Railway opened on August 7, 1873, with a 4ft 8½in. gauge line from St. Helier to Grouville. It was extended to

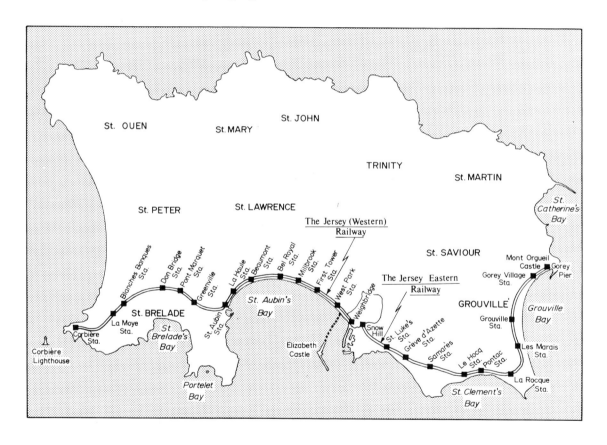

6.4 The Jersey Railways

Gorey Village on August 27, 1873, and to Gorey Pier in 1891. The main terminus was at Snow Hill, St. Helier, and there were stations at St. Luke's, Grève d'Azette, Samarès, Le Hocq, Pontac, La Rocque, Les Marais, Grouville, Gorey Village, and Gorey Pier. The railway was closed on June 21, 1929.

Each company had letter boxes fitted to the guard's vans of its trains. Members of the public could post their letters in the boxes and they were then taken to the Weighbridge or Snow Hill termini, from where they were collected by a postman after the last arrival each evening. Letters were not marked in any way by the railway companies, neither did they bear any special cancellation. It is not known whether the railway companies received any payment from the Post Office for carrying the boxes; all records of the service have been destroyed.

Bags of mail from Gorey, Grouville, La Rocque, and Samarès were carried on the Jersey Eastern Railway's trains and collected at St. Helier terminus by a postman with a hand-cart. At 11 a.m. each day the mail from St. Helier was carried to these sub-offices. A blue pennant was flown from a short mast on the train when mail was on board. No bags of mail were carried by the Western Railway.

Parcels were carried privately by the railway companies and gummed parcel labels or tickets were issued for prepayment. One used by the Jersey Railway about 1910 is illustrated in Figure 6.5. This was for parcels left at the Town Station. Values of 3d., 6d., 8d., and 1s. are also believed to exist.

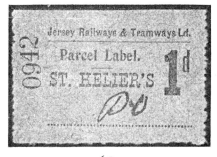

6.5

PARCEL NOTICES

The following notices give parcel rates for the two railways.

THE JERSEY RAILWAYS COMPANY LTD.
PARCEL RATES

Parcels may be left in the Parcel Office "to be called for," at the following rates:—

      1d. per day for Packages not exceeding 28-lbs.

      2d. per day for Packages not exceeding 112-lbs.

Parcels may be forwarded to any Station at the following rates, which must be prepaid, otherwise the Company will not hold itself responsible for any loss or damage :—

Weight not exceeding		4-lbs.	2d.	}	Including delivery within
,,	,, ,,	9-lbs.	3d.	}	a half-mile radius of any
,,	,, ,,	14-lbs.	4d.	}	Station.
				}	Delivered at Station only,
,,	,, ,,	28-lbs.	3d.	}	but if not called for the
,,	,, ,,	56-lbs.	4d.	}	same day the Company
,,	,, ,,	112-lbs.	6d.	}	will not be responsible for
				}	any loss or damage.

Cycles and Bath Chairs . . . 3d.
Perambulators . . . . . 2d.

Parcels can only be delivered between the hours of 9 a.m. and 7 p.m., and the Company cannot undertake to deliver any Parcels on Sundays or Public Holidays.

According to the Post Office Management Act 1837 (1 Vic. cap 33), registered in the Royal Court in Jersey, the Company cannot convey or deliver letters or other communications.

Passengers' luggage, 112-lbs. and under, will be conveyed free of charge; excess weight will be charged at Parcel Rates.

The Company cannot hold itself responsible for any Parcel or Package over £2 in value.

It is particularly requested that all persons depositing or forwarding Parcels with or by the Company will see that they get a numbered ticket of the given value paid, in receipt of same.

NOTE.—Parcels for any particular Train should be handed in ten minutes before the advertised time of starting.

. . . . . .

The date of the notice is not known, but the Jersey Railways Company Ltd. was the title used for the Western Railway from 1883 to 1896. There are pencilled amendments made at a later date which alter the rates of delivered parcels to '3–6lbs. 4d., 9lbs. 6d., and 14lbs. 8d.'

JERSEY EASTERN RAILWAY, 1891
PARCEL RATES

Parcels are conveyed at the following rates, which must be prepaid, otherwise the Company will not hold itself responsible for any loss.

Weight not exceeding 4oz.	1d.	
,, ,, ,, 4-lbs.	2d.	Including delivery within
,, ,, ,, 9-lbs.	3d.	a radius of half a mile of
,, ,, ,, 14-lbs.	4d.	any Station.
,, ,, ,, 28-lbs.	3d.	Delivered at the Station
,, ,, ,, 56-lbs.	4d.	only.

Parcels containing money, properly packed and sealed, insured at:

10s. and under,	2d.	
10s. to £5,	6d.	In addition to parcel rates.
Over £5 up to £10,	1/-	

No parcels over £10 accepted.

Great Western Railway, Guernsey

Typeset labels were locally printed for use on parcels carried by the G.W.R. steamers to other Channel Islands and to England. They are of vertical format, rouletted at top and bottom and imperforate at the sides. They have G.W.R. GUERNSEY in two lines at the top, PREPAID PARCEL reading upwards at the left and STAMP LABEL reading upwards at the right. The value appears in large figures in the centre, with a box below it for insertion of the number of packages. There have been seen the 4d. and 11d. printed in black on white. Others undoubtedly exist.

Southern Railway, Guernsey

Typeset labels were locally printed for carriage of parcels on the company's steamers. An example seen is printed in black on white and has SOUTHERN RLY. in a box at the top, with GUERNSEY in small capitals below it. In a separate horizontal panel across the centre there is the figure of value, 6d., with PARCEL reading upwards to the left of it and PAID reading upwards at the right. In another horizontal panel below it there is a number and below that again is another panel divided into three sections headed 'No. of Pkgs.', 'Weight,' and 'Rate'. Other denominations undoubtedly exist.

Bus Services

Since its foundation in 1923 the Jersey Motor Transport Co. Ltd. has carried parcels on its buses and has issued parcel tickets for pre-payment. These tickets were, and still are, issued in rolls of 500. No details of the first ticket are now available, but there is a certain amount of information on the tickets and rates since 1945.

On October 1, 1945, 3d. black on red and 4d. black on blue tickets were issued and in May, 1947, 4d. and 6d. tickets. On October 4, 1957, a 4d. black on blue parcel label was issued (Figure 6.6). It was printed in rolls of 500 by Williamson, Ticket Printer, Ashton. The top half was stuck to the parcel and the bottom half was signed by the receiving clerk and handed to the sender.

On May 16, 1958, the rates were increased and a 6d. black on green label was issued. This was again printed in rolls of 500 by J. Williamson, Printer, Ashton. It is also a double-ticket with receipt half at the bottom and is very similar to Figure 6.6. It exists with printer's name at bottom and at right-hand side. The service was discontinued in 1969 and the last ticket was a 6d. black on blue.

The parcel rates were as follows:

1945—6lb, 3d.; 12lb, 4d.; 28lb, 6d.; 56lb, 1s.; 1 cwt, 1s. 6d.
1947—12lb, 4d.; 28lb, 8d.; 56lb, 1s.; 1 cwt, 1s. 8d.
1958—12lb, 6d.; 28lb, 1s.; 56lb, 1s. 6d. 1 cwt, 2s.

Up to October, 1960, parcels and newspapers were delivered to any address on a bus route. This meant up to thirty stops on some routes for delivery purposes and was very uneconomic. The service was therefore reorganized and parcels were then delivered only to agents (shops, etc.) close to the bus route. The list of agents was published in the time-table of the Jersey Motor Transport Co. Ltd. It comprised forty-eight names, of which at least six were post offices.

Covers are known prior to World War II which were carried by the buses of the Guernsey Railway Co. Ltd. from St. Sampson's to St. Peter Port and then posted to London on arrival. They bear a 3d. bus ticket and postage stamps to the value of 1½d.

Parcels are only carried on the Guernsey buses nowadays if collected at a bus stop. The charge is prepaid by means of a passenger ticket.

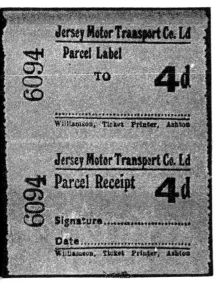

6.6

7

THE SMALLER ISLANDS AND SUB-OFFICES

Alderney

Although post offices were established in Guernsey and Jersey in 1794, no provision was made for Alderney and mail for that island was carried privately until 1812. In that year Sir John Doyle, Governor of Guernsey, wrote to Francis Freeling, Secretary of the Post Office, and offered to arrange carriage of mails by his 'scouts'. Freeling agreed to this and said that he would instruct the Guernsey Postmistress, Mrs. Ann Watson, to make up an Alderney bag whenever required. Some kind of post office was set up on Alderney by Le Messurier, whose family were the hereditary governors.

The arrangement between Doyle and Freeling held good until 1815, when peace was declared between Britain and France, and the carriage of letters reverted to private ships. A private post office is thought to have survived in Alderney after this but no postal markings were used.

In August, 1823, the States of Guernsey passed an Ordinance which set up a special office, known as the Foreign Post Office and run by George S. Syvret and Matthieu Barbet, to handle all mail addressed to or from Alderney and the neighbouring French coast. The masters of all ships were instructed to deliver their letters there and call for mail before sailing. The Ordinance was strengthened later in 1823 and again in 1833 and seems to have been intended to give a monopoly of letters for France and Alderney to one of the private offices still existing and to give official sanction to the position then obtaining, whereby payments of 1d. were made to the master of the ship carrying the letters and the agent at the port. The Ordinance was finally repealed in 1841 but the private post office apparently continued to function for several years afterwards.

On July 21, 1840, a Memorial from the inhabitants of Alderney praying for the establishment of a Government Post Office there was forwarded by the Hon. Fox Maule; also an application from Mr. Brown complaining of the extra charge on letters from Guernsey. The Postmaster General replied on August 5 saying that he could not consent, at present, to make any alterations to the existing arrangements for sending letters to Alderney. It was not until three years later, in 1843, that a post office was established in the island.

The Sub-Postmasters of Alderney were as follows: 1843–74, J. Tilbury; 1874–90, R. Sandford; 1890–1939, A. C. Gaudion; 1939–40 and 1946–54, Col. F. W. Marriette; 1954–1969 Miss L. F. Avdoire (Sub-Postmistress); 1969, Basil Lynn.

7.1

The first cancellation used in Alderney is believed to have been that commonly known as the 'Guernsey Cross' (Figure 7.1). It is extremely rare and there was no reason for it to have been used in Guernsey as the general English type was issued and used there, as it was in Jersey. Channel Islands specialists have as yet no definite evidence to support its use in Alderney, but it can be stated that all but one of the known covers are without contents and only two of the nine recorded and examined bear a Guernsey datestamp. On the other hand, each bears an endorsement 'Via Southampton per private steamer' or similar wording, and has the Southampton Ship Letter stamp on the back. I have seen two letters marked as being written from Jersey, but this does not prove that they were posted there.

The railway had reached Southampton by 1840, but not Weymouth, so it was quicker to send mail via Southampton. A Guernsey Post Office notice allowed this if the letters were endorsed as stated above.

Alderney was a sub-office of Guernsey and most mail passed through Guernsey where it received the ordinary Maltese Cross cancellation and the Guernsey datestamp. Letters were, however, occasionally sent direct to Southampton and it seems probable that the Alderney Postmaster considered that he should cancel such letters before dispatching them and made a special Maltese Cross for this purpose. This was used from 1843 to 1845 until, it is believed, a 324 obliterator of Guernsey replaced it.

7.2

In November, 1847, an undated stamp reading 'ALDERNEY' in sans-serif letters round the top and having two concentric semi-circular arcs at the bottom was introduced (Figure 7.2). A similar stamp with slightly larger letters was sent from the G.P.O. on May 17, 1855. It was not usually used for cancelling postage stamps but was placed on the envelope alongside them and the 324 used as a cancellation.

On May 4, 1848, the numeral obliterator 965 was dispatched from the G.P.O. Two types exist: (*a*) as Figure 7.3, used from 1848 to the mid-1860s; (*b*) with three bars top and bottom, slightly narrower figures, and measuring 22mm across—used from the mid-1860s to 1881. There is also what appears to be a vertical type of this cancellation but evidence has come to light which proves that no vertical 965 was used in Alderney (*see* Chapter 5).

A double-arc datestamp was in use sometime before November, 1853, and there are records of further examples being dispatched from the G.P.O. on July 15, 1855, September 9 and October 23, 1857. Why two examples should have been sent at such close intervals in 1857 remains a mystery, unless the one sent on September 9 never arrived at its destination.

The double-arc datestamp was replaced in 1860 by the small single-circle type 20mm in diameter (Figure 7.4). The P.O. Proof Books record this as having been dispatched on April 27, 1860, and it is known used on May 24 of that year.

This datestamp appears to have been used to cancel postage stamps from 1871 to 1884 and a slightly larger one of 21mm diameter from the end of 1884 until about 1911.

Around the turn of the century a double-circle type came into use (Figure 7.5). It had ALDERNEY at the top and a small cross between thick bars at the bottom. The earliest date of use recorded by the Channel Islands Specialists' Society is July 14, 1897. It started with a letter A above the date but this was removed by 1914. A 'skeleton' type of datestamp 30mm in diameter with ALDERNEY at the top and the date across the centre was used in 1922 and Mr. J. M. Y. Trotter has an example dated October 13.

In the 1930s a double circle with ALDERNEY at the top and CH. IS. between thin bars at the bottom was introduced. This was replaced about 1935 with a similar type with thicker bars and with an asterisk above the date (Figure 7.6).

Round about 1936 a single-circle datestamp 24mm in diameter inscribed ALDERNEY at the top, CH. IS. at the bottom, and with the

7.3

7.4

7.5

7.6

7.7

date in two lines across the centre with an asterisk above it, was introduced (Figure 7.7). It was replaced by a similar-size single circle inscribed ALDERNEY at the top and GUERNSEY CHANNEL ISLANDS at the bottom (Figure 7.8).

A new double-arc type reading ALDERNEY/GUERNSEY CHANNEL ISLANDS was introduced in 1966. It is found lettered A or B. The single circle (Figure 7.8) also continued in use until 1969.

7.8

PARCEL POST CANCELLATIONS

The first parcel post cancellation was a double-ring rubber type with the name ALDERNEY across the centre. It was dispatched from the G.P.O. on July 13, 1911. A similar type reading ALDERNEY/CHANNEL ISLANDS in two lines across the centre (Figure 7.9) is also known on Edwardian stamps but its date of introduction cannot yet be traced. It was probably about 1912–13.

A large label type of parcel post cancellation (Figure 7.10) was issued about 1947. The earliest date of use seen is 1949. A new parcel stamp in the large label type, similar to Figure 7.10 but with ALDERNEY at the top, the date across the centre, CHANNEL ISLANDS at the bottom, PARCEL reading upwards at the left, and POST reading upwards at the right, was introduced in 1958.

7.9

A small circular type used on packets and small parcels is inscribed ALDERNEY GUERNSEY at the top and 'CHAN. ISLES' at the bottom (Figure 7.11). A new rubber stamp similar to this, but with ALDERNEY at the top and CHANNEL ISLANDS at the bottom, was introduced in 1958.

7.10

7.11

MILITARY STAMP

An unusual stamp made of rubber and sent to Alderney on January 30, 1907, is oval in shape and reads POST OFFICE at the top, R.E. OFFICE across the centre, and ALDERNEY at the bottom (Figure 7.12). The R.E. probably stands for Royal Engineers and it seems likely that the stamp was intended to mark military mail posted by the garrison but not to cancel postage stamps.

7.12

AIRMAILS

For details of air flights *see* Chapter 10.

CONCENTRATION CAMP MAIL, 1943–44

During the German Occupation Alderney was completely evacuated of its civilian population, most of whom came to Britain just before the Germans arrived, and was heavily fortified by the Nazis. Russian P.O.W. labour was used and 700 of them are reported to have died following a typhus epidemic.

In August, 1943, 750 French Jews were taken to the island and a concentration camp was established at Camp No. 2 which was called 'Norderney'. The inmates of the camp were allowed to send and receive two letters per month but this privilege was sometimes withdrawn.

Letters were inscribed on the back with the internee's name, personal reference, registered number, hut number, and nature of employment. They then had a 1f.50 Pétain stamp affixed and were handed in at the island office where they were put into sacks and sent by ship to France.

On arrival at Cherbourg the letters were taken to Paris where they arrived at St. Lazare station and were sent to the chief receiving office to be cancelled with the single-line obliterator PARIS CENTRALISATEUR.

Sometimes the mails went via St. Malo or Granville and were taken to Montparnasse station from where, after receiving the circular datestamp of the station, they were delivered in the normal way.

All the letters were censored by the Germans but it is not known whether this was done in Paris or in Alderney. Very few letters have survived.

Covers are known sent by German Occupation forces between 1940 and 1945.

The British post office in Alderney was closed from June 22, 1940, to September 21, 1945. The Army Postal Service provided postal facilities from May to September, 1945, and from that date until September 30, 1946, an officer of the Guernsey Post Office was sent to Alderney and postal services were provided for in the sub-office building. Colonel Marriette resumed his appointment as Sub-Postmaster on October 1, 1946.

SUBMARINE COVER

On May 16, 1947, the submarine H.M.S. Alderney made a voyage to Portsmouth carrying six covers. They bear the Alderney single-circle datestamp of May 16 and the rectangular datestamp COMMANDING OFFICER/16 MAY, 1947/H.M.S. ALDERNEY. The 2½d. postage stamp is cancelled with the Gosport, Hants, datestamp of May 17, 1947.

Sark

Prior to the establishment of a post office in Sark in 1857, letters were carried between the island and Guernsey by boatmen, who usually charged ½d. per letter. Letters are known dated around 1718 but none of them bears a charge mark of any kind.

When Peter Le Pelley was Seigneur of Sark in 1838 he tried to introduce a Post Office and the idea was discussed by the Chief Pleas on several occasions, but it was too revolutionary to be accepted. In those days very few letters were written on the island and most of those were by the Seigneur and the Vicar, and so the boatmen continued to carry the mail in their fishing baskets.

The question was raised again in 1857 and, after long consideration, it was agreed to establish a post office at La Hêche, in a thatched cottage and store belonging to a Mr. Queripel, who became the first Sub-Postmaster. Once a day Mr. Queripel carried the mail from La Hêche to the Creux Harbour and returned with the incoming mail. In the first year of the post office 1,500 letters were posted in

Mr. Queripel's letter box.

According to Leonard Clark in *Sark Discovered*, Mr. Queripel was succeeded by Elie Guille, who had a larger office at New Place, but Guernsey Post Office records contain the following list of successors to Mr. Queripel: 1870–1905, F. Baker; 1905–42, A. Baker; 1942–46, Mrs. E. Baker; 1946–59, W. Carré; 1959–67; Mrs. W. Allen; 1967, Mrs R. Aldridge.

An undated double-arc type of handstamp (Figure 7.13) was dispatched to Guernsey on July 15, 1857, and the first mail left the island on July 21. No example of this first type of postmark has yet been seen on a cover. It would have been struck on the envelope itself and not used to cancel the postage stamps.

7.13

The first datestamp was the single-circle type shown as Figure 7.14. It was probably introduced in 1885 when the Sark post office was created a Money Order Office. It is recorded as being in use by 1890, but does not appear to have been used to cancel postage stamps until 1904. Examples are known used up to 1932. One also exists on a telegram dated 1940.

7.14

A double-circle type was introduced in 1927 (Figure 7.15). It was replaced in the autumn of 1947 by a similar type having an asterisk instead of the A above the date, more space between SARK, GUERNSEY and wider black sectors separating it from CHANNEL ISLANDS (Figure 7.16). This continued until 1966.

On March 17, 1960, a single-circle type of 24mm diameter was put into use with SARK, GUERNSEY/CHANNEL ISLANDS round the circumference and the date in two lines in the centre with an asterisk above.

7.15

A boxed slogan handstamp 50×23mm, reading ISLE OF SARK/1565 CHARTER 1965/QUATER CENTENARY was applied to letters in 1965 (from June 1).

A new double-circle type was introduced in 1966 with SARK at the top and GUERNSEY CHANNEL ISLANDS at the bottom, with thin bars on either side of the SARK. It is lettered A or B above the date.

7.16

LOCAL PARCEL SERVICE

Mails between Sark and Guernsey were carried by vessels of Commodore Cruises Ltd. until 1969, who also ran a parcel delivery service

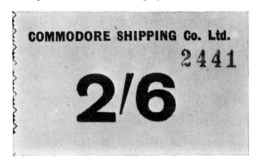

7.17

between the two islands, the parcels being left at one of the Sark stores for collection. It is believed that letters were also carried by this service occasionally after the normal mail from Guernsey to Sark had closed. I have one such cover franked by an imperf. white label inscribed COMMODORE CRUISES LTD./6d./PARCEL RECEIPT—OWNER'S RISK in three lines of black type. The label also bears the serial number 1224 to the right of 6d. It seems likely that the letter may have been tied round with string and handed in as a 'parcel', thus avoiding infringement of the Post Office monopoly.

The Commodore Shipping Co. Ltd. issued adhesives for carriage of parcels from Guernsey to Sark from 1950 to 1969. These are fully detailed in my *Specialised Priced Catalogue of Channel Islands Stamps*. One of the labels is illustrated in Figure 7.17.

The Chausey Islands

The Chausey Islands are situated about eight miles from Granville and twenty-eight miles from Jersey. They are the only remaining French Channel Islands and occupy an area measuring six-and-a-half miles from east to west and five miles from north to south. There are 52 islands at high water and 365 at low water. Several of the larger ones have rough huts on them which serve as temporary shelter for fishermen, but the only permanently inhabited one is La Grande Ile, which is about two miles long and about a mile wide at its greatest width.

Little is known of the early history of the Chauseys but records show that in 1022 they were granted by the Duke of Normandy to the Abbey of Mont St. Michel and that the Benedictines built an abbey on the Grande Ile. A Papal Bull of 1179 confirmed Mont St. Michel in all its possessions including the Chauseys. In 1343 the abbey was taken over by the Cordelier monks and became noted as a seat of learning.

Ancient ordinances of the See of Coutances record the training of several priests at Chausey, but the abbey was finally abandoned in 1543 after raids by Jerseymen.

For the next 200 years the islands remained the abode of smugglers and pirates until in 1737 the French Government built a guard house on the Grande Ile. In 1744 Jersey privateers took possession of the islands and worked the stone quarries there, shipping the stone to Jersey, Guernsey, and Alderney for building fortifications.

In 1755 the French started work on a fort, but in July, 1756, the English landed and destroyed it. In 1765 the French constructed several more forts, and a year later a strong French garrison took up quarters. The Islands have remained in the possession of France ever since.

On December 30, 1780, the Baron de Rullecourt took shelter in the archipelago for six days whilst on the way to attack Jersey.

Today the Grande Ile is a popular resort of day trippers from Granville, St. Malo, Dinard, and Jersey. Boats are chartered from Jersey and have to go to Granville to clear customs.

The island has a substantial farm, a church, a disused fort, two shops, two hotels, a lighthouse, a group of whitewashed cottages, and a château built by Renault, the late French motor magnate.

CACHETS

There is no post office on the island, but there is a letter box from which mail is collected twice a week and taken to Granville for postmarking. A number of rubber cachets have, however, been used during this century and although, like the Tristan da Cunha cachets used up to the end of 1951, they have no official status, they do serve to identify mail posted there. These cachets are applied by the island priest and sometimes by the shopkeepers and hotels.

The first cachet, a double circle with RESTAURANT PIERRE MOULIN round the circumference and 'Iles Chausey' in the centre was used in

7.18

7.19

7.20

7.21

1903 in blue and in mauve in 1905.

The second cachet, a double circle of 25mm diameter reading HOTEL DES ILES/CHAUSEY, was used in 1904, struck in black. A similar type but with 'des' in upper- and lower-case was used in mauve in 1907 and in red in 1913.

The third cachet appears to have been used round about 1910–12 on mail posted on board the twin-screw steamer *Mont St. Michel* which plied between Granville and the Chauseys at that time. It consists of a double-circle rubber stamp, 23mm in diameter, with VAPEUR MONT-St.-MICHEL around the circumference, ILES CHAUSEY LE . . . 19 . . . in three lines across the centre, and a star at the bottom (Figure 7.18). The cachet is struck in a dirty blue on the picture side of postcards and is known on used and unused examples.

An unframed three-line type HOTEL/MOULIN/CHAUSEY was used in violet in 1907. Then followed a large oval with serrated border, reading EXCURSIONS EN MER/PAR LE/VAPEUR POSTAL/ILES CHAUSEY/ GRANVILLE, which was used in violet in 1912 and black in 1913.

In 1920 there was a double circle of 23mm diameter reading ARCHIPEL/HOTEL des ILES/CHAUSEY, struck in violet. Another mark of this period was an oval with HOTEL BELLE VUE/LE PERCHOIS Propre/ ILES CHAUSEY.

Another type (Figure 7.19) consists of a double circle 26mm in diameter containing the words ILES CHAUSEY in serifed capitals in two lines with (Manche) below and a cross at the bottom. It is known in blue or violet used between 1914 and 1922.

Then comes Figure 7.20, which was probably used round about 1930, for it is known cancelling a pair of 50c. Sower issued in 1926. The cachet may have been applied much later, of course, but it is understood that this cachet was in use before the war and has been brought into use again. Its second period of use was in April and September, 1954, and in March, 1955; struck in blue.

Figure 7.21 was used in 1952-54 and again in 1959–60. It is struck in light or dark blue, black or red.

Figure 7.22 was introduced early in 1954. It takes the form of a double circle 48mm in diameter depicting a boat with a sail being rowed by three men across a rather choppy sea, with a five-pointed star above. Between the double circles is the inscription ARCHIPEL DES ILES CHAUSEY. It was struck in light blue or blue-black and was still

7.22

7.23

in use in 1960.

Figure 7.23 was first used in the summer of 1955. It shows a Viking ship and is struck in dull mauve or black up to 1960.

Figure 7.24, struck in red, was used in 1955–57 on board the vedette *L'Albatros*, one of the 'Vedettes Vertes Granvillaises' company's craft which plied between Granville and the Chauseys.

Figure 7.25, struck in dull purple, was used on June 10, 1956, when the Granville Philatelic Society made a special visit to the Chausey Islands.

A boxed type, Service du COURRIER/Iles Chausey-Granville par/ Vedettes Vertes Granvillaises/1er JOUR–La Mouette, was used in blue in 1957. In 1963 a single circle was used on board the vessel *Le President Quoniam*. It reads: SERVICE DU COURRIER/Posté/à bord du/ "LE PRESIDENT QUONIAM"/VEDETTES VERTES/GRANVILLAISES.

Modern hotel cachets are two large circular types for 'Hotel du Fort et des Iles' and 'Blondau, Hotel du Fort' and an oval 'Hotel Belle-Vue, F. Perchey, Propre'.

7.24

7.25
Iles Chausey-Granville par
Vedettes Vertes Granvillaises
"Albatros" - 10 Juin 1956

LOCAL STAMPS

7.26

There have been three local issues for Chausey. On August 7, 1961, a 10c. red featuring a fishing vessel was issued to carry mail to Granville. It was printed in sheets of 12 (3 × 4) rouletted (Figure 7.26). This was banned by the French Post Office in September, 1961.

In 1962 the French company, Vedettes Vertes Granvillaises, issued four denominations: 50c. emerald-green, 1f. dull magenta, 1f.50 orange, and 5f. ultramarine, for carriage of parcels on its vessel *Le President Quoniam* from Granville to Chausey. They were lithographed in Granville and perforated 11½ line (Figure 7.27). These were banned by the French Post Office as they looked too much like postage stamps.

7.27

They were replaced in 1963 by six typeset labels (Figure 7.28) in denominations of 10c. red, 50c. green, 1f. blue, 2f. orange, 5f. red-brown, and 10f. black. These were withdrawn when the shipping contract changed hands in 1966.

Jersey and Guernsey Sub-Offices

The sub-office cancellations can be divided into twelve main types, which are illustrated in Figure 7.29, and the list of offices with their types and periods of use (where known) is given below. *See also* the Notes at the end of the list.

7.28

JERSEY

Augrès. Opened 1869. Types: 2, 3, and 8.

Beaumont. Opened between 1847 and 1854. Types: 1 (in blue 1854, deep blue 1855, dirty green 1857), 3, 4, and 10.

Beresford Street. Opened 1910. Types 3 and 8 (two types). Parcel stamp as Alderney type.

Carrefour Selous. 1891, closed June 30, 1944, re-opened January 1, 1946. Types: 5 and 10.

Cheapside. Opened by 1889. Types: 3 and 8.

Colomberie. Opened 1906; closed April, 1920. Type: 3.

Conway Street. Opened 1874; closed 1910. Type: 3.

David Place. Opened 1874; closed July, 1914. Type: 3.

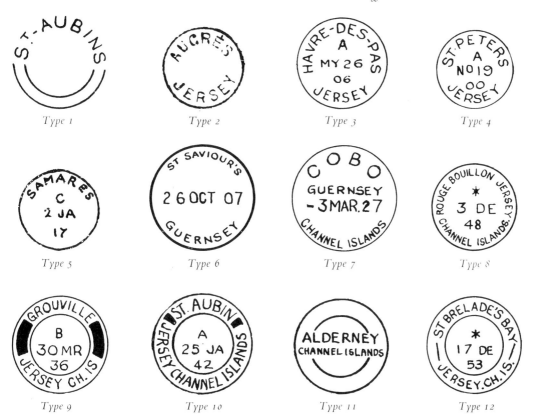

Type 1   Type 2   Type 3   Type 4

Type 5   Type 6   Type 7   Type 8

Type 9   Type 10   Type 11   Type 12   7.29

Faldouet. Opened 1893 (may have been closed for a few years from October, 1919). Types: 5 and 10.

First Tower. Opened 1887. Types: 5 and 8.

Five Oaks. Opened 1891; closed from 1932 to 1937; closed again July 23, 1947, and re-opened April 3, 1950. Types: 3 and 10.

Georgetown. Opened 1882; closed January, 1927; re-opened January, 1935, closed again on June 20, 1940, and re-opened August 22, 1945. Types: 3 and 8.

Gorey. Penny Post, then disappeared until 1852. Types: 1, 3, 5, 10, 11.

Gorey Village. Opened 1896; closed June 20, 1940. Type: 3.

Grands Vaux. Open December 5, 1960. Type: 8.

Great Union Road. Opened 1904; closed January, 1924.

Greve d'Azette. Opened 1927. Types: 3 and 8.

Grouville. Opened by 1854; closed about 1867; re-opened 1891. Types: 1 (in blue), 5, and 10.

Havre des Pas. Opened by 1889. Types 3 and 8.

La Rocque. Opened 1893. Types: 3 and 10.

Millbrook. Opened by 1852; closed January 1, 1944; re-opened September 10, 1945. Types: 1 (in blue 1852, black 1854, blue-black 1855), 3, and 10.

Pier. A temporary office for the acceptance of telegrams was established for the potato season (about six weeks) in 1891. A datestamp was dispatched from the G.P.O. on May 14, 1891. Type: 4.

Pontac. Opened 1902; closed 1904. Type of datestamp unknown.

Quennevais. Opened July 18, 1950. Type: 12.

Rouge Bouillon. Opened 1890. Types: 3 and 8.

St. Aubin's. Penny Post. Called St. Aubin after 1902. Types: 1 (in blue), 2, 3 (three types—St. Aubyns, St. Aubins, and St. Aubin), and 10, skeleton type 30mm diameter, ST. AUBIN, top, JERSEY, bottom, 11 SP 25, centre, and 12.

St. Brelade's Bay. Opened 1891. Types: 3, 6 (purple), and 12.

St. Clement's. Penny Post. Type 1.

St. John's Church. Opened 1891. Types: 5 and 10.

St. John's. Opened by 1853; closed 1867; re-opened 1881; closed January, 1932. Types: 1 (black 1857) and 3.

St. Lawrence. Opened 1855. Type: 1 (black 1857).

St. Martin's. Opened by 1854. Types: 1, 3, and 10.

St. Mary's. Opened by 1856 (also called St. Mary's Church). Types: 1, 3 and 10. This office has a special variety of type 10 in which the name is separated from the rest of the inscription by black circles instead of the usual sectors—thus it can always be distinguished from St. Martin's when only part of the name is showing.

St. Owen's. Opened by 1853. Name changed to St. Ouen's in April, 1922. Before this date both renderings were used. Types: 1, 3, 5, and 10.

St. Peter's. Penny Post, then closed until 1852; closed again on June 20, 1940, and re-opened on September 5, 1945. Types: 1, 4, 8, and 10. Also two skeleton types.

St. Saviour's. Penny Post but no later record.

Stopford Road. Opened July, 1914. Type: 8.

Samares. Opened 1889. Types: 5 and 10.

Sion. Opened January, 1932. Type: 10.

Town Mills. Opened 1904; closed October, 1921. Type: 3.

Trinity. Penny Post; closed by 1867; re-opened 1891. Types: 1 (dark blue 1857) and 10.

GUERNSEY

Bouet Road. Opened by 1889; closed by 1893.

Braye Road. Opened 1938; closed February 9, 1943; and re-opened May 1, 1947. Type: 8.

Camp du Roi. Opened 1925; closed July 1, 1940. Type: 10.

Câtel. Opened by 1850; closed June 19, 1940; re-opened May 1, 1953. Types: 1 (black 1859), 5, and 8.

Cobo. Opened 1889. Types: 6 (purple and black), 7, and 10.

Forest. Opened 1893; closed 1896 and re-opened 1902. Types: 6 (blue, purple or black), 7, and 10.

La Moye. Opened 1891; closed 1896.

La Valle. Penny Post, no later record.

L'Islet. Opened 1889; closed June 29, 1940; re-opened November 1, 1945. Types: 3, 6 (purple), and 10.

Les Baissieres. Opened February 1, 1952. Type: 8. Now closed.

Les Gravées. Opened by 1891. Types: 3 and 8.

Market Place. Opened by 1887; closed September 21, 1942; re-opened December 17, 1945. Types: 3 and 8 and a parcel stamp.

Mount Row. Opened by 1896. Type: 6 (purple). Closed in 1900s.

Pleinmont Road. Opened 1958. Closed 1965. Type: 8.

Quay B.O. Opened June, 1932; closed September, 1939; re-opened September 1, 1948; closed May 30, 1953. Types: 8 and 10.

Rocquaine. Opened July 11, 1967. Closed 1969. Type: 8.

St. Andrew's. Opened 1889; closed March 26, 1943; re-opened 1946. Types: 3, 5, and 10.

St. John's. Opened January, 1935; closed June 22, 1940; re-opened July 8, 1948. Type: 8.

St. Martin's. Opened by 1850; closed 1867; re-opened 1887. Types: 1 (black 1855, dark blue 1858), 3, and 10.

St. Peter's. Opened by 1852; closed 1867; re-opened 1878. Name changed to St. Peter-in-the-Wood by 1891. Types: 1 (black 1855, greenish-blue 1856), 3, 5, and 10.

St. Sampson's. Opened by 1850. Types: 1 (red 1853, blue 1857), 5 (several variations), 8, 10, and 11. Parcel stamp 1954.

St. Saviour's. Opened 1906. Types: 6 (purple) and 10.

The Vale. Opened 1896 (formerly called La Valle?). Types: 5 and 10.

Torteval. Penny Post, then no record until 1911: closed June 21, 1940; re-opened April 13, 1946. Type: 10.

Vale Road. Opened 1896; closed June 22, 1940; re-opened December, 1, 1945. Types: 3, 8, and 10.

Ville au Roi. Opened January, 1936; closed June 30, 1942; re-opened February 2, 1948. Type: 8.

Herm. Opened May 1, 1925; closed November 30th, 1938. Type: 10.

Notes

1. All cancellations are in black unless otherwise stated.

2. The types illustrated are main types but some of the datestamps vary slightly from them though not always enough to justify listing as sub-types. For instance, type 3 can be found with the name of the island at the bottom with or without the letters C.I. and in two sizes, 22mm and 24mm in diameter.

3. Type 2 is found on the early registration labels and not usually cancelling stamps.

4. Types 8, 10, and 12 vary somewhat—'Channel Islands' may be in full or abbreviated, according to the length of the sub-office name.

5. Type 11 for *Gorey* and *St. Sampson's* shows the parish name without 'Channel Islands'.

6. Rubber datestamps in type 6 are recorded in the G.P.O. Proof Books as having been supplied for *Sark, St. Peter's,* Jersey, *St. Martin's,* Jersey, and *Les Gravées,* but I have not yet seen examples of them used.

7. Type 11 is recorded in the G.P.O. Proof Books reading *Market Place Guernsey* in two lines, but this has not yet been seen used.

8

CHANNEL ISLANDS – FRANCE MAILS

Postal History

Prior to 1843 letters were carried privately between the Channel Islands and France and were handed to agents on either side of the Channel for onward transmission. As explained in Chapter 1, the agent would hand them to the captain of a ship who, in turn, would hand them to another agent at the port of arrival. For this service a fee of 3d. (or 3 decimes in France) was charged, 1d. going to each agent and 1d. to the captain of the ship. A list of agents was given in Chapter 1.

THE FOREIGN POST OFFICES

By Ordinance of the Royal Court of Guernsey dated August 23, 1823, a Foreign Post Office was set up in Guernsey for the purpose of dealing with letters to and from Alderney and the neighbouring coast of France. Two Guernseymen, Georges S. Syvret and Matthieu Barbet, held the monopoly of this service, making a charge of 2d. per letter, payable by the addressee, 1d. of which went to the Master of the ship bringing it. The Ordinance was twice confirmed, first on December 13, 1823, and again in March, 1833, and was not repealed until January, 1841; thus for eighteen years the Royal Prerogative was infringed with impunity.

According to a report made by George Louis, a Post Office Surveyor, who visited Jersey in 1829, a similar office (known as the French Post Office) was functioning there. It was run by one Theodore Fontaine, and was concerned with the collection and dispatch of mails between St. Helier, Granville, and St. Malo.

Louis believed this office to be sanctioned in some way by the French Government. A letter in my possession leads me to believe that this office was in fact an official agency of the French Post Office.

The letter was written by Theodore Fontaine on May 4, 1842, to the Director-General of Posts, Paris, and requested 'that as he (Fontaine) had to dispatch express packets every day to the Postmasters of St. Malo and Granville which called for the use of large quantities of wrapping paper, could he be supplied with some for the use of his office, also some wax'.

It reads:

Jersey, le 4 mai 1842.

Monsieur Le Directeur Général,

Ayant chaque jour, et souvent plusieurs fois par jour, à adresser des paquets de dépêcher à MM. Les Directeurs de St. Malo et de Granville, ce qui exige une certaine quantité de papier pour emballage et par conséquent m'oblige à de frais, je vous serai reconnaissant de vouloir bien m'en envoyer pour l'usage de mon bureau, ainsi que de la cire.

TH. FONTAINE.

On the front of the letter is the address and the word Service, also the red Outremer-St. Malo datestamp of 4 Mai 1842 (as Figure 8.16); inside is yet another datestamp, this time in blue and reading Cabinet Particulier (Postes) 6 Mai 1842.

Both Foreign Post Offices were officially suppressed on June 1, 1843, in consequence of a new Anglo-French Postal Convention which came into force on that date. Under this Convention all mail to or from France was to be delivered to the British Post Office, and the French Postal Authorities agreed that it should not be sent through any other channels. Neither of the Foreign Post Offices used any postal markings.

THE POSTAL CONVENTIONS

The Postal Convention of 1843 provided for official exchange of mail between various British and French ports and for Packets between the Channel Islands and St. Malo. It also provided for mails to be

86

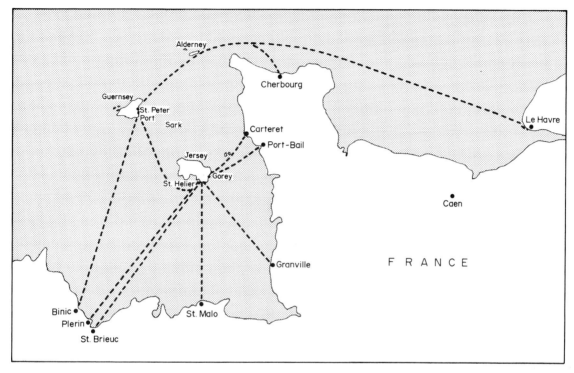

8.1 Shipping routes

carried by private steamers between Jersey and Guernsey and Cherbourg, Granville, and St. Malo (*see* map in Figure 8.1). The service between Jersey and Cherbourg was suppressed in 1845. Rates of postage were 5d. per $\frac{1}{2}$ oz from England and 3d. per $\frac{1}{2}$ oz from the Channel Islands. This was the rate to the French port of arrival and an additional 5 decimes per $\frac{1}{4}$ oz was added for the French inland rate.

The Convention also provided for *boîtes mobiles* (movable boxes) in which letters could be posted and cancelled at the port of arrival. At a number of English ports special handstamps bearing the framed letters M.B. were applied to letters, but although it seems likely that similar ones were issued to the Channel Islands none has so far been recorded. On the French side, however, letters from the Channel Islands were marked with a small circular datestamp reading ILES-C at the top and bearing the name of the port, Cherbourg, Granville or St. Malo at the bottom. The 'c' stands for 'Channel', a curious mixture of French and English.

Two covers are known from this service. One is from Jersey to France and has a single G.B. 1855 4d. on blue paper cancelled with the 3176 small-figures lozenge of St. Malo and the ILES–C ST. MALO c.d.s. of January 8, 1856. The other cover is addressed from Jersey to St. Malo. It bears a pair of the G.B. 1855 4d. on blue paper cancelled with the 1441 small-figures lozenge of Granville and the ILES–C GRANVILLE c.d.s. of May 10, 1856.

In January, 1855, the rate of postage from both the Channel Islands and England was standardized at 4d. per $\frac{1}{2}$oz. The 4d. letter was therefore a single one and the 8d. a double letter.

In 1856 a new Anglo-French Postal Convention was signed which provided for another boîte mobile service, of which full details are given later in this chapter. This service came into force on January 1, 1857, and continued until the outbreak of war in 1939. Rates of postage were: 1855–June 30, 1870, 4d. per $\frac{1}{2}$ oz; July 1, 1870–December 31, 1875, 3d. per $\frac{1}{2}$ oz; January 1, 1876–June 11, 1921, $2\frac{1}{2}$d. per 1 oz; June 12, 1921, 3d. per 1 oz. It is interesting to note that the 1856 Convention reduced the rate from England to France from 6d. to 4d. but abolished the reduced Channel Islands rate of 3d.

THE P–F AND P–D HANDSTAMPS

As a result of the 1843 Convention, P–F and P–D handstamps were issued to the Jersey and Guernsey post offices. Letters going beyond France could only be prepaid for the English and French postage— hence P–F (Paid to Frontier). The marking P–D indicates Paid to Destination.

It is probable that Jersey had a P–F stamp but no example has yet been recorded. The oval P–D stamp (Figure 8.2) was used from 1843 to 1862 and is known struck in red, black, blue, and a dirty green. The circular P–D stamp (Figure 8.3) was used from 1863 to 1875, generally in black, occasionally in red. In 1875 a small oval type (Figure 8.4) was struck in black or red. It had sloping letters without the hyphen between them. A replacement for this was sent from the G.P.O. on July 16, 1879.

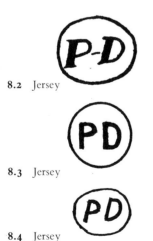

8.2 Jersey

8.3 Jersey

8.4 Jersey

Guernsey had an oval P-F stamp (Figure 8.5) in use in 1843–44, which was struck in dull red. An oval P-D stamp (Figure 8.6) was in use from 1843 to 1856, struck in red at first and then in the colour of the datestamp. It was damaged at the top. The circular P-D stamp (Figure 8.7) was used from 1856 to 1874 and was struck in the colour of the datestamp, blue or black. The oval P-D stamp, with break at the top, is also known in black on a cover from Guernsey to St. Malo dated August 12, 1872.

Letters to France from Jersey and Guernsey via Calais and Boulogne in 1856–57 are known with a larger circular P-D stamp with thicker letters and in 1866 with a smaller type. These were probably applied in London. Some of these covers have a large handstruck PAR LONDRES. This was privately applied by P. Beghin of Jersey.

8.5 Guernsey

8.6 Guernsey

8.7 Guernsey

Pre-Adhesive Markings

The first marking known to have been used on letters from the Channel Islands is D'JARSEY, unframed and measuring 21 × 3mm, applied at St. Malo to a letter from Jersey dated July 17, 1683 (Figure 8.8). This mark appears to have been little used, as only two examples are known.

Another marking found is D'ANGLETERRE struck in black from 1699 to 1720 and used on letters from England as well as from the Channel Islands. This was followed in 1720 by a larger ANGLETERRE which can be found struck in red, blue or black until 1802. From 1802 letters routed via England are found marked ANGLETERRE PAR BOULOGNE (or CALAIS or ROUEN) in two lines in black or red, and letters going direct from the Islands to the nearest French ports have GRANDE BRETAGNE PAR CHERBOURG (or GRANVILLE or ST. MALO) in two lines in black (Figure 8.9). This latter mark was used on letters from the Channel Islands only. The St. Malo mark is found with a damaged G in GRANDE after about 1830.

Other markings found on letters from Jersey and Guernsey, but not, of course, restricted to letters from those islands, are:

SMALO in black measuring 27 × 4mm on letters from Guernsey, dated 1776 and 1777 (Figure 8.10).

D'JARSEY
8.8

GRANDE BRETAGNE
PAR GRANVILLE
8.9

SMALO
8.10

ST MALO

8.11

34 ST SERVAN

8.12

PAYS D'OUTREMER

8.13

ST-MALO
13
MARS
1836
(34)

8.14

ST. MALO in black, measuring 28 × 3½mm on a letter from Guernsey dated 1790 (Figure 8.11). There also exists 34 ST MALO in two lines in black, measuring 5 × 3½mm and 28 × 3½mm on a letter from Guernsey, dated 1793.

GRANVILLE in black, measuring 36 × 4mm (the G is slightly larger and measures 6mm) on a letter from Jersey dated 1781. The 34 ST. SERVAN in two lines, measuring 8 × 5mm and 38 × 5mm exists on a letter from Guernsey dated 1817 (Figure 8.12).

34 ST. SERVAN (as above) with 'Colonies par' written in manuscript above it on a letter from Sark dated 1819.

DEB 48/CHERBOURG in two lines (1815); DEB 34/ST. MALO in two lines (1828–30); P34P/ST. MALO (1828–31); MORLAIX (1816); 48/CHERBOURG in two lines (1823–29).

COLONIES PAR ST. MALO (or CHERBOURG or GRANVILLE or LE HAVRE) in black or red between 1760 and 1830; a framed COL. PER CHERBOURG used in 1815 (one of the rarest French pre-adhesive marks); and a framed PAYS D'OUTREMER in black or red about 1830 (Figure 8.13) used in conjunction with datestamps (Figures 8.14 and 8.15). All these stamps are the French equivalents of the British ship letter stamps.

Small circular datestamps, 20mm in diameter, struck in black or red and reading OUTRE-MER at the top and GRANVILLE (or ST. MALO or LE HAVRE) at the bottom, with the date in three lines across the centre (Figure 8.16) were brought into use in 1839 and are found on letters from the Channel Islands as well as from many other places abroad. A distinctive mark, similar in size to the Outremer datestamp but worded ILES-C at the top (Figure 8.17) was introduced in June, 1843, and was struck in red (a strike in black is known dated March 12, 1850) and remained in use until about 1879. The ports at which it was used were Cherbourg, Granville, and St. Malo. Cherbourg is very rare.

Another mark especially made for use on letters from Jersey and Guernsey was a flat-topped 3 indicating the 3 decimes ship charge due and struck in red at Granville and St. Malo (Figure 8.18).

Handstruck 6, 7, and 8 decime marks can be found on letters from Jersey and Guernsey. They are usually struck in black and denote the amount of postage due.

Letters from the Channel Islands are also occasionally found with the ANGL. CALAIS and ANGL. BOULOGNE datestamps, having been routed via London and Dover across the Straits.

Note: The dates given for the introduction of the various hand-struck markings are those recorded in the *Catalogue des Estampilles et Oblitérations Postales de France et des Colonies Françaises* (Yvert, 1929) and *Marques Postales de la Manche 1698–1876* by L. Dubus and J. de Micoulsky (1945).

8.15

The Boîte Mobile Service

Under Article II of the Postal Convention between Great Britain and France dated September 24, 1856, in addition to the regular mail service, letters were to be exchanged between several British and French ports, such mails being carried by private vessels of either country, a gratuity of 1d. being paid on each letter. This means of communication became so constant that all the vessels carried movable boxes on board for collecting such letters, and stamps were brought into use for postmarking letters so posted.

8.16

The steamers of the London & South Western Railway ran from St. Helier to St. Malo and Granville on alternate weekdays, carrying the regular mails between the Islands and France. They also carried a movable letter box (boîte mobile) in which letters, which had not passed through the post office, could be posted up to the time of sailing, and afterwards by passengers on board. On arrival at the destination these boxes were taken to the post office, where the letters were removed for cancelling.

There appears to have been no Guernsey movable box on this service. Letters were carried direct to St. Malo from Guernsey for many years by the *Fawn*, a 47-ton cutter. The captain was given letters by the post office and also received them from private persons. These letters when cancelled at St. Malo received the M.B. stamp. There is no evidence that the cutter *Fawn*, or the steamer by the same name, had a movable box on board. Mr. Trotter has a number of 1849–54 letters from Cherbourg to Guernsey, all unstamped, some carried privately, probably by the *Alerte*, Captain Fortin, others through the post office via Granville and St. Malo. Postage paid was 8d. (5d. French $\frac{1}{4}$ oz, 3d. English $\frac{1}{2}$ oz).

8.18 Decimes mark

8.19   8.20   8.21 Granville   8.22 Le Havre   8.23 St. Malo

8.24 Granville

8.25 Le Havre

8.26 St. Malo

Letters from Jersey and Guernsey had the British stamps cancelled with the normal French numeral obliteration, and in addition the covers received a dated postmark, at first octagonal (Figure 8.19) and later circular (Figure 8.20), reading ANGL. B.M. GRANVILLE (or LE HAVRE or ST. MALO). The numeral obliterator consisted of a combination of four figures in a lozenge of dots (Figures 8.21 to 8.23). Small figures were used at first but when the French post offices were renumbered on January 1, 1863, larger figures were introduced (Figures 8.24 to 8.26). The numbers were as follows:

				Small Figures	Large Figures
Cherbourg	..	..	..	842	1002
Granville	..	..	..	1441	1706
Le Havre	..	..	..	1495	1769
St. Malo	..	..	..	3176	3734

The most common cancellations are those of St. Malo, and the rarest those of Cherbourg. Entire covers from Granville and Le Havre are scarce. Mails to Cherbourg and Le Havre probably went by French ships from Guernsey.

For many years from the end of the nineteenth century the *Courier* ran a monthly service between Guernsey, Alderney, and Cherbourg, carrying mails. Mr Trotter has only seen letters sent to England via Cherbourg by this service. These have no French stamps and were perhaps transferred direct to an English mailboat. The Postmaster General's Report for 1898 reports the start of a service to Alderney from Southampton via Cherbourg every Tuesday. The mail was transferred to a smaller vessel (probably the *Courier*) in Cherbourg harbour and mail from Alderney was handed over for passage back to Southampton.

Unpaid letters of 1858–59 and 1870 are known with French 8 and 6 handstruck marks in black. These denote the number of decimes due at double rates and are extremely rare.

8.27

The lozenge obliterations went out of use in April, 1876, and after that date the ordinary town datestamps were used. About 1906 a large single-circle type was brought into use at St. Malo; this reads ANG. B.M. SAINT-MALO and has the date in two lines across the centre with a star above (Figure 8.27).

Letters from the French ports were cancelled on arrival at St. Helier with a 'milestone' type worded JERSEY FRANCE MB with the date in two lines below (Figure 8.28). The 'milestone' was dispatched from the G.P.O. on March 24, 1857. The earliest recorded date of use is April 26, 1858.

A similar stamp (Figure 8.29) was sent to Jersey on July 25, 1873. It had larger lettering and the letters M.B were wider spaced with a stop between them. The latest date of use recorded is August 24, 1939.

8.28

When this cancellation was issued it had straight sides but continous use from 1873 caused the sides to become distorted as shown in the illustration. Examples dated before 1914 have the month placed before the day, after that year the day preceded the month.

French stamps up to the 'Peace and Commerce' issue are found cancelled with the 409 numeral obliterator of Jersey, and the 'milestone' is struck on the cover. Later issues are found cancelled with the 'milestone'. (Both types of cancellation are known on the 'Peace and Commerce' stamps.)

The Proof Book in the P.O. Record Room records that an M.B. datestamp was sent to Guernsey at the same time as the Jersey one was dispatched but so far no stamps or covers bearing this mark have been found. French stamps were cancelled with the 324 numeral obliterator or with a Guernsey datestamp.

8.29

French stamps with Jersey and Guernsey cancellations are much rarer than British stamps cancelled in France.

The boîte mobile service ceased at the outbreak of World War II in 1939 and is unlikely to be restarted. A photograph of an actual boîte mobile appears in Figure 8.30.

Lists of British stamps with French cancellations and French stamps with Channel Islands cancellations follow. I am greatly indebted to the late Leslie G. Tomlinson for assistance in compiling the British

8.30

list. It is not claimed that either list is complete and further information would be welcomed.

BRITISH STAMPS WITH FRENCH CANCELLATIONS

(a) *Figures in lozenge of dots*

Cherbourg 1002 (large figures)
1867–80 3d. rose. Plates 5 and 6.

Granville 1441 (small figures)
1856–58 1d. rose-red, wmk. Large Crown, P.14.
1856–58 2d. blue, wmk. Large Crown, P.14. Plates 5 and 6.
1855–57 4d. pale carmine, wmk. Small Garter.
1855–57 4d. rose, wmk. Large Garter.
1855–57 6d. lilac, wmk. Emblems.

          1706 (large figures)
1856–58 1d. rose-red. Reserve Plate 15.
1858 1d. rose-red. Plates 138, 158, 210.
1862 4d. pale red.
1865–67 4d. dull vermilion. Plates 7, 10.
1867–80 3d. rose. Plates 5, 6, 7, 8, 9.
1867–80 1s. green. Plate 4.
1873–80 3d. rose. Plates 12, 14, 15, 16.
1872–73 6d. chestnut. Plate 11.
1873–80 1s. green. Plate 8.

Le Havre 1495 (small figures)
1847 10d. brown.
1856–58 1d. red-brown.
1854–57 1d. red-brown, wmk. Large Crown, P.14.
1856–58 1d. rose-red.
1855–57 4d. rose, wmk. Large Garter.
1855–57 6d. lilac.
1858 2d. blue. Plates 7 and 8.

          1769 (large figures)
1856–58 1d. red.
1858 1d. red. Plates 71, 74, 81, 83, 91, 127, 129, 184.
1858 2d. blue. Plate 9.

1869   2d. blue. Plate 13.

1862   4d. red. Plates 3 and 4.

1865–67 4d. vermilion. Plates 9 and 10.

1867   1s. green. Plate 4. Cancelled in red and believed to be the only copy so cancelled.

1867–80 3d. rose-red. Plates 5 and 6.

1867–80 6d. mauve. Plate 9.

St. Malo   3176 (small figures)

1854–57 1d. red-brown, wmk. Large Crown, P.14.

1854–57 1d. red-brown, wmk. Large Crown, P.16.

1854–57 2d. blue, wmk. Large Crown, P.14. Plates 5 and 6.

1857   4d. wmk. Large Garter, all shades.

1856   6d. lilac.

1862   4d. pale red and 4d. red.

3734 (large figures)

1856–58 1d. rose-red, wmk. Large Crown, P.14.

1856–64 1d. red. Plates 71, 74, 82, 84, 85, 86, 87, 88, 91, 92, 93, 94, 95, 97, 100, 118, 129, 134, 137, 151, 168, 175, 183.

1858   2d. blue. Plate 9.

1869   2d. blue. Plate 13.

1862   4d. red and pale red. Plates 2 and 4.

1865–67 4d. vermilion. Plates 7, 8, 9, 10, 11.

1867–80 3d. rose. Plates 5, 6, 7, 8, 9, 10.

1867–80 6d. lilac. Plate 6. 6d. dull violet. Plate 8.

1870 $\frac{1}{2}$d. rose and rose-red. Plates 6 and 9.

1873   6d. grey. Plate 12.

1873–74 3d. rose. Plates 11, 12, 14.

1875   3d. rose. Plates 16 and 17.

(b) Datestamps

Granville (round)

1868   4d. vermilion. Plate 10.

1876–80 2$\frac{1}{2}$d. rosy-mauve. Plates 2, 3, 4, 6, 8, 11, 13, 14, 16.

1877   4d. sage-green. Plate 16.

1880–81 $\frac{1}{2}$d. deep green.

1880–83 2$\frac{1}{2}$d. blue. Plates 17, 19, 20, 22, 23.

1883   2$\frac{1}{2}$d. lilac. (Two sizes of datestamp.)

1887   ½d. vermilion.
1887   2½d. purple on blue.
1902–10 ½d. yellow-green.
1902–10 2½d. blue.
1911   K.G. V 1d. red.

Le Havre (octagonal)
1865–67 4d. vermilion. Plate 11.
1873–80 6d. grey. Plate 17. Cancelled in red.
1876–80 2½d. rosy-mauve. Plate 15. Cancelled in red.
1880–83 2½d. blue. Plate 23. Cancelled in red.
        (round)
1880   4d. grey-brown. Plate 17.
1880–83 2½d. blue. Plate 23.

St. Malo (round)
1876–80 2½d. rosy-mauve. Plates 2, 3, 4, 7, 11, 12, 13, 15, 16, 17.
1880–83 2½d. blue. Plates 18, 19, 20, 22, 23.
1881   1d. lilac. 16 dots.
1883   2½d. lilac. (Two sizes of datestamp.)
1887   2½d. purple on blue.
1902–10 ½d. yellow-green; 1d. scarlet; 2½d. blue.
1902–10 1d. scarlet. (1906 type datestamp, Figure 8.27.)
1912–22 3d. violet.
1935   2½d. ultramarine. (1906 type datestamp, Figure 8.27.)
1937   red, 1½d. brown. (1906 type datestamp, Figure 8.27.)

FRENCH STAMPS WITH CHANNEL ISLANDS CANCELLATIONS

Guernsey 324
1853–61 40c. orange.
1870   Bordeaux 10c. yellowish-bistre.
1862–71 20c. blue.
1862–71 40c. orange.
1876   30c. cinnamon, Peace and Commerce.
1877–90 Peace and Commerce, 10c. black on lilac, 25c. black on rose.
1872–75 30c. grey-brown.

Datestamp
1877–90 Peace and Commerce, 10c. black on lilac, 25c. black on rose.
1903   Sower 15c. green (dated April 10, 1925).
1907   5c. green, 10c. brick-red.
1926   Sower 50c. vermilion.

Jersey 409
1853–61 20c. blue.
1853–61 40c. orange.
1862–71 10c. bistre, 20c. blue, 30c. deep brown, 40c. orange.
1862–71 80c. rose-red.
1870   Bordeaux, 5c. green, 10c. bistre, 20c. blue, 20c. pale blue,
    30c. deep brown.
1862–70 Laureated Head 30c., 80c.
1870–73 5c. green on blue.
1872–75 15c. yellow-bistre.
1872–75 30c. grey-brown.
1876   Peace and Commerce 25c. blue.
1876   Peace and Commerce 5c. green, 10c. black postcard, 30c.
    cinnamon.
1877–90 Peace and Commerce 25c. black on rose, 25c. ochre on
    yellow.

Datestamp (squared circle)
1877–90 Peace and Commerce 25c. ochre on pale yellow.

Datestamp (c.d.s.)
1907   Sower 25c. blue (dated August 19, 1912).

Machine Cancellation (seven wavy lines)
1937   Peace 1f. carmine-pink; 1938 Mercury 25c. green.

'Milestone' M.B.
1877–90 Peace and Commerce, 4c. purple-brown on grey, 5c. green
    on pale green, 15c. blue, 25c. black on rose, 25c. ochre on yellow.
1900   Blanc 2c. claret, 5c. blue-green.
1900   Mouchon 15c. orange, 25c. blue.
1900   Merson 1f. lake and yellow-brown.
1902   Mouchon redrawn 10c. carmine, 25c. blue.

97

1903   Sower 10c. rose-carmine, 25c. blue.

1907–13 Sower 5c. deep green, 10c. brick-red.

1925–36 Sower 25c. ochre-brown, 40c. violet, 40c. ultramarine, 45c. violet, 50c. sage-green, 50c. vermilion.

1926–27 90c. on 1f. 05 vermilion.

1927   Berthelot 90c. rose-carmine.

1924   Olympic Games 25c. deep and dull carmine.

1929–33 90c. magenta.

1930   Air 1f.50 blue.

1932–39 75c. sage-green, 90c. scarlet, 1f. 25 carmine.

1934   Cartier 1f. 50 blue.

1935   Normandie 1f.50 sky-blue.

1936   Ampere 75c. brown.

1937   Paris Exhibition 1f.50 greenish-blue.

1937   Descartes 90c. scarlet.

1937   Ceres 2f.25 ultramarine.

1938   Champagne 1f.75 bright blue.

1938   Arc de Triomphe d'Orange 2f. sepia.

1938   Royal Visit 1f.75 bright blue.

1939   New York World Fair 2f.25 bright ultramarine.

1939   Photographic Centenary 2f.25 blue.

PAQUEBOT MARKS

PAQUEBOT

8.31

A PAQUEBOT handstamp of the omnibus type, Studd A1, was used in Jersey in the mid-1900s (Figure 8.31). Examples are known in black dated 1903 and in violet dated 1905 on postcards bearing French 'Blanc' type stamps cancelled with the Jersey–France 'milestone' M.B. stamp.

Three types of the mark exist: Type 1 measures 6 × 40mm and was struck in black in 1903–04 and in violet in 1904–05. Type 2 measures $4\frac{1}{2} \times 34$mm and was struck in violet in 1905. Type 3 measures $4\frac{1}{2} \times 30$mm and was struck in violet in 1905. Types 1 and 2 have sloping letters and type 3 has upright letters.

In 1970 two postcards with a French Mouchon 10 centimes red cancelled with the Guernsey squared circle of August 21, 1903, were discovered with a violet PAQUEBOT measuring $4 \times 34\frac{1}{2}$mm, which also appears to have been applied in Guernsey. Its main point of difference

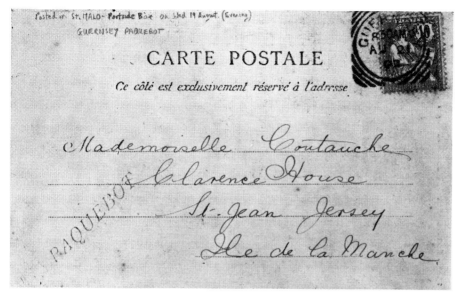

Posted in St. MALO- Portable Box on Wed 19 August (Evening)
GUERNSEY PAQUEBOT

CARTE POSTALE

Ce côté est exclusivement réservé à l'adresse

PAQUEBOT

Mademoiselle Coutauche

Clarence House

St. Jean Jersey

Île de la Manche

8.32

from the Guernsey mark is in the tail of the Q which is much rounder (Figure 8.32).

Other Ports

There are four other ports that cancelled mail from movable boxes, but I can find no reference to them in the 1857 Convention or its later additions.

PORT–BAIL

Port-Bail is situated on the west coast of the Cotentin peninsula and from about 1868 to 1885 letters were sent there from Gorey. A circular datestamp similar to Figure 8.20, with PORT-BAIL at the bottom, is known on a letter from Jersey on April 14, 1869, which arrived the next day. A G.B. 1868 3d. rose, plate 5, is known with the Outremer/Port-Bail datestamp of May 4, 1871.

Another cover is known with a 3d. G.B. stamp with the Jersey duplex cancellation of November 7, 1874, and the Port-Bail arrival stamp of November 9, 1874.

Apart from the two covers mentioned, only about half-a-dozen loose stamps are known with Port-Bail markings. These are listed in the table below.

Little is known about the steamer services between Gorey and Port-Bail, but it is believed that letters were usually carried by summer excursion steamers and that the service was by no means regular. The port became silted up in 1885 and the steamer service ceased.

PLÉRIN

Plérin, in the Bay of St. Brieuc, is another port at which mail from the Channel Islands was occasionally landed. It had a B.M. c.d.s. similar to Figure 8.20 in 1872 and an example is known on a G.B. 3d. rose on cover from Guernsey. An 1880 2½d. blue is known on cover from Jersey (cancelled with the Jersey squared-circle datestamp of October 13, 1885, and bearing the Plérin/Cotes du Nord arrival stamp of the same day) (Langlois collection).

BINIC

Binic, another small port in the Bay of St. Brieuc near Plerin, also received mail from the Channel Islands. Sailings were made from Guernsey by the cutter *Reindeer*, owned and commanded by Captain J. G. Piprell, and later by his new vessel, the *Echo*. For a number of years in the early twentieth century the *Fawn*, belonging to the St. Malo and Binic Steamship Co. Ltd., also made regular sailings to the port. Pierre Langlois has a part cover from Guernsey to Binic dated 1872 and bearing a pair of the 1858 1d. red cancelled with the '480' large-figures lozenge of Binic. A number of postcards from Guernsey to Binic are known. Each bears an Edward VII stamp cancelled with the Binic/Cotes du Nord datestamp of 1907–08. An oval B.M. stamp is applied to each card.

CARTERET

The little port of Carteret is situated on the west coast of the Cotentin peninsula, near to Port-Bail. From about 1900, letters were carried from Gorey by the vessels of the Compagnie Rouennaise de Navigation, the paddle-steamers *Cygne* and *Jersey*. In recent years letters have been carried by the *Torbay Belle* and *Les Deux Léopards*, belonging to the Compagnie Navigation Carteret, but only if they bear French stamps.

Two types of cancellation are known on British stamps used on postcards routed via Carteret. The first consists of three concentric circles, the outer one being made up of dots, with the word CAR-TERET at the top, MANCHE at the bottom, and the date in three lines in the centre. Examples are known from 1903 to 1908. The second type consists of a single circle 26½mm in diameter, with CARTERET at the top, MANCHE at the bottom, and the date in three lines in the centre. Examples are known used from 1908 to 1913. Two types of PAQUE-BOT stamp are known used on the cards: both are of the French omnibus type. The first measures $4\frac{1}{2} \times 30\frac{1}{2}$mm and was used from 1903 to 1912. The second measures 4×30mm and was used in 1912–13.

For a number of years ordinary bags of mail were also carried between Jersey and Carteret and letters to and from France are known with the Carteret transit mark.

ST. BRIEUC

For a number of years in the late nineteenth and early twentieth centuries there were regular shipping services between the Channel Islands and St. Brieuc, in the Cotes du Nord. It seems likely that mail was carried on these services and British stamps with the '3533' large-figures lozenge and with later St. Brieuc datestamps may possibly exist.

The British stamps known with the cancellations of the above ports are:

Port-Bail
1865–67 4d. vermilion, plate 8—2984 lozenge (large figures).
1868   3d. rose, plate 5—Outremer–Port-Bail datestamp of May 4, 1871.
1868   3d. rose, plate 6—2984 lozenge (large figures).

1875   3d. rose, plate 16—2984 lozenge (large figures).
1879   2½d. rosy mauve, plate 15—Port-Bail datestamp of September 7, 1879.

Plérin
1867–80 3d. rose—ANGL. B.M./PLERIN datestamp of July 12, 1872.

Binic
1858   1d. rose-red (Plate No.)—480 lozenge (large figures).
1902–10 1d. scarlet—Binic datestamp of 1907–08.

Carteret
1902–10 ½d. blue-green—triple-circle datestamp.
1902–10 ½d. yellow-green—triple-circle datestamp.
1902–10 1d. scarlet—triple-circle datestamp.
1902–10 2½d. blue—triple-circle datestamp.
1911   ½d. yellow-green—single-circle datestamp.
1911–12 ½d. yellow-green—single-circle datestamp.

9

THE GERMAN OCCUPATION

The Channel Islands were occupied by German Forces from July 1, 1940, to May 8, 1945.

Jersey Swastika Overprint

The first philatelic result of the Occupation was the overprinting of British stamps found in Jersey with a swastika and 'JERSEY 1940'. Orders were given to the acting postmaster, Mr. O. F. Mourant, by the German Commandant, Captain Gussek, to supply quantities of stamps for overprinting and these were taken to Messrs. Bigwoods, printers to the States of Jersey, with an official order for the work to be carried out. A Post Office receipt form signed by Bigwoods Ltd. states that the firm has received stamps to the value of £22 4s. 2d. for the purpose of overprinting. It is dated July 20, 1940. Proofs were first made on the 1940 Postal Centenary issue (all values except the 1d., which was not available) by means of a small swastika and type carved from wood. There was only one block available, so each stamp had to be overprinted separately.

Next a swastika was cast, the rest of the inscription was set up in type, the whole re-cast, and formes made for the overprinting. The 1938 King George VI ½d., 1½d. 2d., 2½d. 3d., 4d., 5d., 6d., 7d., 8d., 9d., 10d., and 1s. were overprinted in a forme of 60 and the Postal Centenary ½d., 1½d. 2d., 2½d., and 3d. were overprinted in a forme of 40. Four of each of the 2s. 6d., 5s., and 10s. were also overprinted.

Whilst this was being done the Bailiff of Jersey protested to the German Commandant against this defacing of the King's head and the matter was referred to Berlin for guidance. As it was the policy

9.1   9.2

of the Germans to treat the Channel Islanders as courteously as possible, the issue was not proceeded with and orders were given for the stamps to be destroyed. Two sets to the 1s., however, escaped destruction and both are in the hands of British collectors. One set, consisting of the ordinary and Centenary stamps and some proofs of the Centenary issue, is in the hands of the author and two values are illustrated in Figures 9.1 and 9.2. The other, consisting of the ordinary and Centenary stamps, is in the collection of Mr. E. Hirsch. A few other odd values are also in existence.

Guernsey Overprint

9.3

Stamp Collecting of December 22, 1945, records the following story from Mr. Frank C. Graham of Effingham: 'When the now famous "bisects" of British 2d. stamps were projected the Nazi Military Governor of Guernsey conceived the idea of adding a swastika in the form of an overprint on each half stamp. Specimens so treated were actually forwarded to Germany for approval, but the proposal was promptly and emphatically vetoed on the grounds that the overprint would deface the portrait of a reigning monarch. Strict instructions were issued that all the trial stamps were to be destroyed. Needless to say, however, a few examples escaped, and our informant was told that three copies have been given to a small girl in the Island by a German soldier and that one had positively been seen by a local collector, who was unable to acquire it.'

Two 2d. Postal Centenary stamps are known with a small swastika struck twice on each. These were probably part of the experiment.

During a Commando raid on Guernsey in 1940 some 1d. King George VI stamps as illustrated in Figure 9.3 were found and brought back to Britain. Some were sent to me by a man who went on the raid.

Jersey 1d. Essays

At the same time as the British stamps were overprinted some local 1d. stamps were prepared by Bigwoods. They were designed by R. W. Cutland and show the Arms of Jersey (or more correctly the

Arms of the King of England which were given to the Bailiffs of Jersey and Guernsey by King Edward I in 1279 in the form of official seals) surrounded by a belt containing the words 'Etats de Jersey'. They were printed in scarlet in sheets of 30 (10 × 3) on white wove unwatermarked paper, and are known with and without a swastika and '1940' overprint rather similar to that which appeared on the British King George VI stamps but without the word JERSEY (Figure 9.4).

Three imperforate sheets of each type existed. Two of each were

9.4

9.5

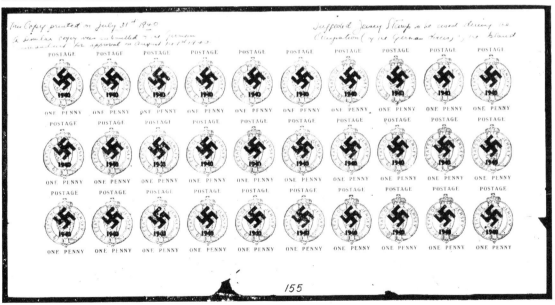

broken up and sold to various collectors. A complete sheet without overprint is in the National Postal Museum and one with overprint from my collection is illustrated in Figure 9.5. Like the overprinted British stamps, they were not issued. It is interesting to note that they are inscribed 'States of Jersey' although the Post Office was still being run by British officials as part of the British Postal Service.

German Official

Another interesting item from the early days of the Occupation is a label (Figure 9.6) said to have been used by Captain Gussek, the first

9.6

German Commandant of Jersey, on his official correspondence. It is printed in black and cancelled in red with the handstamp of Dienst-stelle 22006. It is possible that the label is of the same status as the Afrika Korps and Inselpost stamps and was issued to German soldiers to control the number of parcels that they sent back to Germany.

The Bisects

Once the Germans were in occupation no further supplies of British stamps were obtainable and after a few months supplies of the ½d.

and 1d. stamps began to get low. The situation was more acute in Guernsey than in Jersey and it was therefore decided to produce some stamps locally and work on an issue was started in October 1940. By December, however, supplies of the British 1d. were so low that they became exhausted before the local product was ready. The German authorities therefore suggested that the 2d. stamps should be bisected diagonally and used as 1d.'s. This procedure was adopted and on December 24, 1940, the following Post Office notice appeared in the *Evening Press* and *The Star*:

NOTICE

The Post Office advises that further supplies of 1d. Postage stamps are not at present available and that, until further notice prepay-

9.7

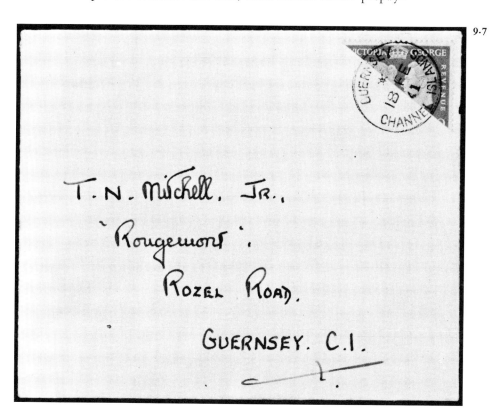

ment of Penny Postage (for Printed Papers, etc.) can be effected by **using one half of a 2d stamp** provided that **division is made by cutting the stamp diagonally**.

It is emphasised that the bisection of stamps should be done carefully and that correspondence bearing half stamps not cut in the manner indicated will be liable to surcharge.

Although the bisecting was authorized on Christmas Eve, the mails had by then been collected and the stamps were not cancelled until December 27, as the previous two days were public holidays.

Four different stamps were bisected, the ordinary King George VI 2d. and the Postal Centenary 2d. (Figure 9.7) which were on sale at all post offices, and some King George V 1912-24 and 1934 2d.'s, which were in the hands of private collectors but still valid for postage. It has been estimated that the following quantities were used: George V 1912–24, 600; George V 1934, 500; George VI 1938, 16,000; Postal Centenary, 100,000. They remained valid until February 22, 1941, but were cancelled on the 24th for mail received up to midnight on the 22nd.

Many of the bisects were used philatelically by collectors who sent them to themselves or their friends. Those used by local government departments and firms to send out bills and receipts are worth considerably more than the 'made-to-order' covers.

UNAUTHORIZED BISECTS

Only the 2d. bisect was authorized, but at least one example of the $2\frac{1}{2}$d. is known bisected and used as 1d. Several examples of the ordinary 1d. and the Centenary 1d. are also known bisected and used as $\frac{1}{2}$d. stamps.

The Occupation Stamps: Guernsey

When the decision was made in October, 1942, to issue locally produced postage stamps in Guernsey the Guernsey Press Company was approached to undertake the work and Mr. E. W. Vaudin, the firm's artist, was asked to prepare a design. The Germans would not allow the stamps to bear the King's head or any connection with Britain, so Mr. Vaudin used what are commonly called the Arms of Guernsey, but which are in fact the personal Arms of the Sovereign of England, and the unsuspecting Germans let him get away with it.

He first prepared rough sketches and then made finished drawings approximately 76×70mm ($3 \times 2\frac{3}{4}$ in.) on Bristol board.

After the drawing had been approved, Mr. Charles H. Toms prepared the printing plate of 30 subjects for the 1d. stamp. From this plate sheets of 60 were typographed in two operations, the top half of the sheet first, then the bottom half. Some sheets can be found with the fifth and sixth rows out of alignment because the automatic printing machine has failed to line up the paper properly. The paper used for the first printing of the 1d. and part of the second was pre-war Samuel Jones paper already gummed. That used for all other printings and values was locally gummed.

The $\frac{1}{2}$d. and $2\frac{1}{2}$d. stamps were prepared in the same way, but the sheets of 60 were printed in one operation from two joined plates of 30.

The 1d. stamp was issued on February 18, 1941, and the press notice authorizing it read as follows:

NOTICE—POSTAGE STAMPS

As from 9.0 a.m. on TUESDAY, the 18th inst., penny postage stamps will be available for purchase at the Head Post Office, Smith Street, and at all Sub-Offices in the Bailiwick where Money Order or Savings Bank business is normally transacted.

The present arrangement whereby 2d. stamps, cut diagonally, provide for penny postage will cease on Saturday, the 22nd instant.

H. C. CHAPELL, *Acting Head Postmaster.*

Post Office, Guernsey,
17th February, 1941.
Genehmigt (Approved)
Nebenstelle Guernsey
der Feld Kommandantur 515
    I.V. DR. BROSCH
Kriegsverwaltungs—Assessor
den 17 Febr. 1941.

The ½d. stamp appeared on April 7, 1941, after publication of the following notice:

NOTICE—POSTAGE STAMPS

As from 9.0 a.m. Monday, the 7th April, locally printed Halfpenny Postage Stamps will be on sale at the Head Post Office, Smith Street, and at all Sub-Offices where Money Order or Savings Bank business is transacted.

H. C. CHAPELL,   Acting Head Postmaster.

Post Office, Guernsey.
1st April 1941.
Genehmigt (Approved)
Nebenstelle Guernsey
der Feldkommandantur 515
(Verw.) DR. REFFLER
Kriegsverwaltungsrat.
den 1 April, 1941.

The 2½d. was issued unheralded on April 12, 1944, on German orders as an economy measure to save paper. Sales were restricted to ten copies per person.

A full list of the major varieties appears below.

LOCALLY PRINTED ISSUES 1941–44

Arms of Guernsey (Figure 9.8). Designed by E. W. Vaudin. Typographed by Guernsey Press Co. in sheets of 60 (6 × 10). Rouletted 7 (or 14 due to blunt points). No watermark. [Catalogue numbers are from the *Specialised Priced Catalogue of Channel Islands Stamps*.]

9.8

(a) White paper

9. ½d. emerald-green (April 7, 1941)
    a. imperf. between stamp and bottom margin
    b. imperf. between vertical pair (6 pairs exist)
    c. imperf.
10. ½d. blue-green (November, 1941)
    a. offset
    b. imperf. between horizontal pair (less than 10 pairs exist)
11. ½d. yellow-green (February, 1942; November, 1944)
    a. imperf. between horizontal pair (20 pairs exist)
    b. offset
12. ½d. sage-green (September, 1942)
    a. imperf. between horizontal pair
    b. imperf. between stamp and top margin
13. ½d. olive-green (February, 1943)
    a. deep olive-green
14. ½d. deep yellow-green (July, 1943)
    a. printed on gummed side (60 exist)

15. 1d. scarlet—thin paper (February 18, 1941)
    a. imperf. between horizontal pair (less than 10 pairs exist)
    b. offset
20. 1d. scarlet—thick paper (February 18, 1941)
    a. double printing (*see* Figure 9.9)
    b. imperf. between vertical pair (10 pairs exist)
    c. imperf. between stamp and margin
    d. imperforate (4 complete sheets, 240 stamps, exist)
21. 1d. vermilion (July, 1943)
22. 1d. orange-vermilion (July, 1943)
23. 1d. carmine-red (December, 1943)

24. 2½d. deep ultramarine (July, 1944)
    a. imperforate
25. 2½d. ultramarine (April 12, 1944)
    a. imperforate (mint strip of 3 known; one used copy known, probably from a partly perforated sheet)

9.9 Double print

(b) *Blue banknote paper, watermarked loops*

26. ½d. grass-green (March 11, 1942)
   a. on greenish-blue paper
27. 1d. carmine (April 9, 1942)
   a. on greenish-blue paper

Forgeries?

A number of ½d. and 1d. stamps are known on a thin transparent paper and differing considerably in shade, roulette, and gum from the printings of 1944 from which they purport to come. Three ½d. imprint blocks in deep yellow-green, another block in a paler green, and a fifth block in an olive-green have been seen, together with a 1d. imprint block resembling that from the 15th printing (described on page 115), but with much narrower margin, and two other blocks in deep red.

These stamps have been shown to Mr. E. J. Baker, and compared with his extensive stock, and he considers them to be forgeries. They have also been submitted to the designer, Mr. E. W. Vaudin, formerly of the Guernsey Press Co., who writes:

I have examined the stamp specimens very carefully and it is difficult to tell in the actual printing if these are genuine, but in this matter there is one detail which practically satisfies me that these are forgeries. In each of the 1d. stamps the back legs of the two leopards are broken.

What is more convincing is the rouletting. Your specimens were made with wheels in perfect condition, whereas, as I have already stated, the wheels on the machine at the "Press" were very worn, besides being a different size.

The whole production of the stamps was rouletted at the Press Co. I do not believe that at the time any other firm here had a similar machine, all used the round hole punch perforators.

The gum on the back looks too perfect. After the first, and part of the second printing, our stock of gummed paper ran out, and for every consecutive printing the paper had to be gummed by hand. This was done, after trial of various methods, by the slow and laborious method of brushing the gum with a 4-inch brush and laying out each sheet to dry. The difficulty of obtaining adhesive solution was another problem. Crystal gum arabic melted down and mixed with dextrine was first used and later liquid gum arabic was obtained from France.

At a glance I would have taken these stamps as genuine, but on close examination I think you can definitely state that these are not from any of the official printings.

It has been suggested that these stamps may have been made by the British Government for espionage purposes, like the similar issues they made for France, Germany, Italy, and the Netherlands. It has also been suggested that they were reprints made after the war, when further supplies of paper and fresh rouletting wheels were available, but that their sale was banned by the Postmaster General. I do not know what the answer is, but the stamps definitely do not match up with any of the official printings, and the roulette wheels have never been used by the Guernsey Press Co. The Herm locals printed by the same firm have been rouletted with wheels similar to those used throughout the Occupation. One thing can be said for certain, these 'forgeries' are very much scarcer than the issued stamps, and I have seen no large blocks of them.

Presentation Sheets
Unnumbered sheets of the first printing of the ½d. and 1d. values were presented to the Bailiff by the Guernsey Press; also the 2½d. imperforate. These can be classed as proofs. A single mint copy and three used ones (two on cover) of the 2½d. imperforate are in my collection.

Offsets
Some of the ½d. and 1d. stamps are known with reversed impressions of the designs on the back. They were caused by the design from a wet-inked sheet transferring to the back of the succeeding sheet, or by a sheet of paper missing in the printing machine and the impression being taken by the underlay and then transferring to the back of the next sheet.

In March, 1942, a printing of the ½d. and 1d. was made on paper with an overall watermark of loops and the word ARMA. It had been imported from France and was intended for printing currency notes.

In fact, a number of local 6d. and 1s. notes, and possibly some of the higher denominations, were actually printed on this paper. The ½d. stamp was issued on March 11, 1942, and was completely sold out by the 31st and the 1d. was issued on April 7 and was completely sold out by the 25th.

Plate flaws
Some of the more prominent plate flaws are:

Halfpenny
Stamp No. 25.   Outer frame-line bent.
          43.   Break at top left of outer frame.
          48.   Break in bottom right corner of outer frame-line.
One Penny
          21.   Break at bottom right of outer frame-line below value tablet (from April, 1942, printing).
          51.   As above.
Twopence-halfpenny
One stamp has been seen with the top outer frame-line very badly broken. It is not constant but probably came from the final sheet printed.

Numbers printed
The following were printed:
½d., 1,772,160; 1d., 2,478,700; 2½d., 416,640; watermarked paper, ½d., 120,000; 1d., 120,000.

Imprints
The imprint of the Guernsey Press Company appeared on every printing. It is found under stamps 55 and 56 on the first printing of the 1d. and under stamps 57 and 58 on all other printings of the 1d., ½d., and 2½d. The imprints on all sheets up to December, 1943, are similar to the illustration (Figure 9.10). They reveal the name of the printer (Guernsey Press Co.), the number of the issue, the quantity printed (120M = 120,000), the date of the printing. After December, 1943, only the printer's name was given, the other data being omitted. Even this was finally reduced to PRESS TYPE or 'PRESS'. The full list of imprints is as follows:

Guernsey Press Co., 6 x 240M/11/41

9.10   Imprint block

114

1d.

1, 120M/2/41; 2, 2 × 120M/2/41; 3, 3 × 120M/6/41; 4, 4 × 120M/6/41;
5, 5 × 120M/9/41; 6, 6 × 240M/11/41; 7, 7 × 120M/2/42; 8, 8 × 240M/
4/42; 9, 9 × 240M/9/42; 10, 10 × 240M/1/43; 11, 11 × 240M/7/43;
12, Guernsey Press Co.; 12 (second half), PRESS TYPE; 13, "PRESS" (inverted commas unlevel); 14, "PRESS" (inverted commas level);
15, "PRESS" (inverted commas level—bottom margin 12mm).

½d.

1, 240M/3/41; 2, 2 × 120M/6/41; 3, 3 × 120M/6/41; 4, 4 × 120M/11/
41; 5, 5 × 120M/2/42; 6, 6 × 240M/2/42; 7, 7 × 120M/9/42; 8,
8 × 120M/2/43; 9, 9 × 120M/7/43; 10, 10 × 120M/10/43; 11, Guernsey
Press Co., (stop and comma); 12, Guernsey Press Co. (stop only);
13, Guernsey Press Co. (stop only—bottom margin 15mm).

2½d.

1, Guernsey Press Co.; 2, "PRESS" (inverted commas unlevel);
3, "PRESS" (inverted commas level); 4, "PRESS" (inverted commas level
—bottom margin 15mm).

The Occupation Stamps: Jersey

Jersey's first Occupation stamps were copied from the Guernsey 1d.,
a sheet of which was sent over to Major N. V. L. Rybot for him to
use as the basis of his design. He first prepared drawings approximately 114 × 101mm (4½ × 4 in.) for the 1d. and 140 × 127mm
(5½ × 5 in.) for the ½d. In each corner of the 1d. he put a small letter A,
which he has since revealed stood for 'Ad Avernum Adolf Atrox'
('To hell with you atrocious Adolf'); in the upper corners of the ½d.
he placed the letter A, and in the lower corners the letter B, which
stood for Atrocious Adolf and Bloody Benito. (*See* Figures 9.11
and 9.12.)

9.11.

The stamps were typographed by the *Jersey Evening Post* in sheets
of 60, and the plates were prepared in a similar way to those of
Guernsey.

The 1d. stamp was issued on April 1, 1941, and the ½d. on January
29, 1942. Brief announcements of the impending issue of these two
stamps were made in the *Jersey Evening Post* on March 31, 1941, and
January 27, 1942, but no P.O. notices appear to have been published.

9.12

There are no shades of any consequence, but there are four different varieties of paper: thin, thick, newsprint, and chalky. The thin paper can be distinguished by the design showing through the back; the newsprint is greyish in appearance; the chalky can be distinguished by its very shiny surface and its thick appearance. It also passes the silver test.

A list of major varieties follows.

LOCALLY PRINTED ISSUES 1941–42

Arms of Jersey (Figures 9.11 and 9.12). Designed by Major N.V.L. Rybot. Typographed by *Jersey Evening Post* in sheets of 60 (6 × 10). Perf. 11 on various papers. No watermark. [Catalogue numbers are from the *Specialised Priced Catalogue of Channel Islands Stamps*.]

21. ½d. bright green—thick paper (January 29, 1942)
    a. imperf. between horizontal pair (less than 10 pairs exist)
    b. imperforate (one sheet of 60 stamps exist)
    c. imperf. between stamps and top margin
    d. double horizontal perfs.
22. ½d. bright green—thin paper (August, 1942)
    b. dark green
    c. extra row of perfs. across stamp
23. ½d. green—grey newspaper
    b. imperf. between vertical pair

24. 1d. scarlet—thin paper (April 1, 1941)
    a. carmine
    b. imperf. between horizontal pair (less than 10 pairs exist)
    c. imperf. between vertical pair (12 pairs exist)
    d. extra vertical rows of perfs.
25. 1d. scarlet—thick paper
    b. extra row of horizontal perfs.
26. 1d. scarlet—chalky paper (October, 1941?)
27. 1d. scarlet—grey newspaper (January, 1943)

Imprints
All printings of the 1d. had the imprint "Evening Post" Jersey 17/3/41 below the first three stamps in the bottom row, and all sheets of the

9.13 Imprint block

½d. the imprint "Evening Post," Jersey, January, 1942 in the same position (Figure 9.13).

Plate flaws
Double-frame varieties are known, but they are of little consequence as they were caused through over-inking. Plate varieties can be found on nearly every stamp in the sheet, and with a little patience it should be possible to plate them.

Some of the most prominent are:

Halfpenny
Stamp No. 1, 2, 3, 5, 8, 10, 16, 18, 30, 37, 43, 47, left-hand value tablet incomplete.

2. Two lions have each only one eye.
6. Full stop under fraction of ½ in right-hand tablet.
9. Middle bar of second E of JERSEY broken.
14. Vertical bar across S of POSTAGE.
25. Break in bottom left-hand corner of frame.
36. Bottom lion has long claw extending into S of POSTAGE, and 2 in right-hand value tablet is thinner than normal.

45.   Broken P of POSTAGE.
48.   White circle alongside Y of JERSEY.
49.   Break in bottom row of pearls beneath A of POSTAGE.
50.   White stop over GE of POSTAGE.

One Penny

Stamp No.   1, 2, 3, lions with only part of mouth.
5.   White spot to left of J of JERSEY.
13.   Full stop under serif of right-hand 1.
29.   Break in centre of bottom outer frame-line.
30.   White spot after Y of JERSEY.
31.   Bottom lion has missing eye.
37.   Each lion has missing eye.
42.   White circle alongside right value tablet.

Numbers printed

The following numbers were printed: ½d., 750,000; 1d., 1,000,000.

1943 PICTORIALS

Early in 1943 it was decided to issue a set of pictorial stamps showing views of Jersey, and Edmund Blampied, a well-known Jersey artist, was approached to prepare the designs, for which he was paid £10 each by the Post Office.

Blampied's drawings were unsuitable for direct reproduction as stamps. They were, therefore, sent to Paris with instructions that fresh drawings, suitable for reproduction, be made by a French artist. Monsieur Henri Cortot copied Blampied's drawings, partly by hand and partly by photography, and from these copies the actual stamps were prepared. The Blampied drawings are now in the Post Office Archives and the Cortot ones in my collection (*see* Figures 9.14 and 9.15).

Essays

Essays were prepared half the size of the issued stamps, some on India paper and some on wove paper. The following are known: ½d. black, ½d. chrome-yellow, ½d. red, ½d. steel-blue, ½d. dull purple, ½d. cold violet, ½d. turquoise-green (wove), ½d. green and black,

9.14 Blampied's drawing (actual size 178 × 127mm).
Note small lettering, three rows of beading, and
EB initials

9.15 Cortot's drawing from which stamp was engraved
(actual size 95 × 76mm). Note larger lettering,
two rows of beading, names of designer and
engraver. Margin contains pencilled instructions

½d. sepia and brown, ½d. pale green and red, ½d. maroon; 1d. pink and maroon, 1d. maroon, 1d. blue and maroon, 1d. yellow and maroon (India). Besides differing in size and colour, these essays differ from the issued stamps in the following respects: on the ½d. there are three ornamental lines beneath the picture instead of two, and the initials 'E.B.' appear one on each side of the value in the place of the name 'Blampied' underneath 'Jersey' (Figure 9.16). The design of the 1d. essay is as issued.

9.16 Half-size essay

Die proofs
Four die proofs of each value were struck in black on a very rough grey paper and signed by Cortot.

Colour proofs
Colour proofs of each value were made and four or five of each exist in the following colours:

½d. green (as issued)	1d. ochre.
½d. orange.	1½d. brown (as issued).
½d. maroon.	2d. brown-orange.
½d. red.	2d. orange (as issued).
1d. green.	2½d. blue.
1d. blue.	3d. deep violet.
1d. deep violet.	3d. violet (as issued).

Some were signed by Cortot.

Black presentation proofs
Six proofs of each value were struck in black on a better quality white wove paper but were not signed. They were intended for presentation to Jersey officials but were evidently not claimed.

Epreuves-de-luxe
As with all modern French issues, 100 sets of the Jersey pictorials were printed in the issued colours for presentation to various officials. Each value was printed imperforate in the centre of a thin card measuring 121 × 146mm (4¾ × 5¾ in.) and having at the bottom a puncture of a half moon between two diamonds. The holes were punched by the automatic accounting system of the French P.T.T. The imprint 'Atelier de Fabrication des Timbre-Poste. PARIS.'. appears in the

lower right-hand corner in the same colour as the stamp. Each of these *epreuves-de-luxe* is covered with tissue paper.

9.17 Issued stamps

The Stamps

The stamps were printed at the French Government Printing Works, Paris, in the following designs (Figure 9.17): ½d., Old Jersey Manor Farm; 1d., Portelet Bay; 1½d., La Corbière; 2d., Elizabeth Castle; 2½d., Mont Orgueil Castle; 3d., Gathering vraic (seaweed) near La Rocco tower, St. Ouen's Bay. The Royal Cypher GR was worked into the design of the 3d. on each side of the value. All designs incorporate the names Blampied and Cortot. The stamps were perforated 13½.

The stamps were in sheets of 120, consisting of four panes of 30 (ten rows by three). Before dispatch to the post offices they were separated into P.O. sheets containing two panes of 30 side by side.

Press announcements of the issue appeared in the *Jersey Evening Post* on May 31, June 7, and June 29, 1943. They were issued in three pairs, the ½d. and 1d. on June 1, 1943, the 1½d. and 2d. on June 8, 1943, and the 2½d. and 3d. on June 29, 1943.

Corner dated blocks

The sheets had the same markings as the normal French stamps and dated corner blocks exist. The date appeared in the bottom right-hand corner of the sheet.

Printings and Quantities
[Catalogue numbers are from the *Specialised Priced Catalogue of Channel Islands Stamps*]

No.	Value	Corner dates known		Quantity	
28	½d.	1.5.43	3.5.43	360,000	on white paper
		6.10.43		120,000	on grey paper (resembling newsprint)
29	1d.	7.5.43	8.5.43	360,000	on white paper
		7.10.43		240,000	
		28.2.44		240,000	on newspaper
30	1½d.	17.5.43	18.5.43	360,000	on white paper
31	2d.	20.5.43	21.5.43	360,000	on white paper
32	2½d.	31.5.43		360,000	on white paper
		25.2.44		360,000	on newspaper
33	3d.	4.6.43	5.6.43	360,000	on white paper

The Jersey Post Office paid the French Government Printing Works a total of £548 7s. 8d. for the work.

Inter-Island Mails

The carriage of mails between Guernsey and Jersey was restarted by the Germans on July 10, 1940. Some letters were delivered in the sister island the day after posting, others took a month or two to arrive. These mails were seldom censored, but on one occasion they were taken from Guernsey to Paris for examination and were then sent on to Jersey. After the Allied landings in Normandy mails were sometimes censored at the German Feldposts in the Islands.

Provisional Registration Marks

Registration continued in both islands throughout the Occupation, but eventually the adhesive registration labels ran out and it was impossible to obtain further supplies from Britain. Locally made handstamps were therefore used.

In Jersey, from the middle of 1943, when large numbers of first-day covers of the French-printed pictorials were being sent, an unframed handstamp consisting of the letter A, B or C and a three- or four-figure number was struck in blue. The few examples seen have all been on covers dated June 29, 1943, but according to the Head Postmaster of Jersey, the use of this handstamp continued until the end of the Occupation. It seems likely, however, that at some of the sub-offices, where the volume of registered letters was much smaller, adhesive labels lasted much longer than at the head office.

In Guernsey, from 1944, a framed handstamp was used. It had GUERNSEY at the top and was struck in violet. A serial number prefixed by the letter R was inserted in red at the bottom.

When the Sark registration labels ran out in 1944 some of the pre-war Herm ones were used there provisionally. Mr Trotter has an example and I have one with Herm deleted and Sark written in manuscript.

Cancellations

To the best of my belief, no cancelling stamps were made locally during the Occupation, but in both islands locally made year figures 41, 42, 43, 44, and 45 were used in the handstamps and in the date-stamps attached to the cancelling machines (*see* Chapter 4). In Guernsey the 0 in the cancelling machine datestamp was bisected vertically and half used as a 1 during 1941.

The sub-offices open during the Occupation were:

GUERNSEY

Braye Road (closed February 9, 1943), Cobo, Forest, Les Gravées, Market Place, St. Andrew's (closed March 26, 1943), St. Martin's, St. Peter-in-the-Wood, St. Sampson's, St. Saviour's, Sark, The Vale.

JERSEY

Augrès, Beaumont, Beresford Street, Carrefour Selous (closed June 30, 1944), Cheapside, Faldouet, First Tower, Five Oaks, Gorey, Greve d'Azette, Grouville, Havre des Pas, La Rocque, Millbrook (closed January 1, 1944), Rouge Bouillon, St. Aubin's, St. Brelade's Bay, St. John's Church, St. Martin's, St. Mary's, St. Ouen's, Samares, Stopford Road, Sion, Trinity.

Franks

Postage stamps became exhausted at various times in both islands and letters sent during those periods can be found with either 'PAID' machine or handstamps or with meter stamps. Full details will be found in Chapter 4.

Jersey Mail Cancelled in France

Montmartin-sur-Mer is a small fishing village six miles south-west of Cherbourg in the Department of Manche.

On August 12, 1940, a German Field Post Office arrived from Jersey and set up headquarters in the village; with it came a quantity of Jersey civilian mail comprising about 1,500 letters and 200 packets, which had not been cancelled in the Island. Not knowing what to do with it, the Germans handed it over to the French postmistress. She, thinking of the many English families awaiting news, cancelled all the letters with the normal Montmartin s/mer datestamp and forwarded them with the French mail. She took this step entirely on her own initiative and without receiving instructions from a higher authority.

9.18

It seems probable that most of the covers from Jersey have been destroyed by the recipients. However, one piece exists and it is illustrated in Figure 9.18.

Details of the cancellation are as follows:

Single circle, 26mm in diameter, with MONTMARTIN S/MER at the top, MANCHE at the bottom, and the time and date in three lines across the centre, 18, 12–8, 40.

I am greatly indebted to the Postmistress of Montmartin-sur-Mer for supplying information from the official records.

The German Feldpost

Field Post Offices were opened by the Germans in Guernsey and Jersey on January 8, 1941. All civilian mail to the Continent went through these offices. The Jersey Feldpost was in Falle's shop in Beresford Street and the Guernsey one at Le Jardinet, St. Martin's. All mail to Germany, France, Belgium, Netherlands, and Italy had to be sent via the Feldpost at a charge of 25pf. for letters and 15pf. for postcards.

Letters from Guernsey were taken by the Germans to Granville, where a 1f.50 French stamp was affixed and cancelled and the letter sent on to its destination by the French Post Office. Two letters dated August, 1941, from the Head Postmaster of Guernsey to Bordeaux have German Hindenburg stamps cancelled with the datestamp of Feldpost 843. Alfred Clements, in his book *The German Fieldpost, 1937–45*, records this as having been in Paris, and later elsewhere in France, but it is possible that it was attached to a unit in Guernsey for a short while in 1941 because the Channel Islands were administered from France.

The number of the Feldpost is believed at one period to have been 319, but I have seen no covers bearing that number. Those known definitely to have originated in Guernsey, apart from the two mentioned above, have a small letter 'e' above the date and a bar where the number should be.

I have seen several covers with German stamps cancelled with the normal Guernsey datestamp. The Postmaster of Guernsey informed me that one or two were cancelled inadvertently at the G.P.O. instead of at the Feldpost. Letters could be handed in at either the G.P.O. or the German Feldpost.

In Jersey, German stamps were used from the start of the service. The earliest one in my possession is addressed to the Chief Officer of the s.s. *Spinell*, c/o Mr. Joult, Feldkommandantur 515, Granville, and has a British stamp cancelled Jersey, February 13, 1941, two German stamps cancelled in mauve with the Feldpost datestamp of

13.2.41 with three short bars in place of the number, and a French stamp cancelled Prisonniers de Guerre, Paris, 6.3.41. Some cards and letters dated 1941 and 1943 have German stamps cancelled with the Feldpost datestamp without number and French stamps cancelled at Granville.

Letters were sent either by air or by speedboat and may bear either 'Mit Luftpost/Par Avion' labels or a boxed cachet in red reading 'Mit Schnellboot/befördert'.

I have one from Jersey to Berlin with a Jersey 1d. stamp cancelled in violet with a small oval cachet reading 'Jersey-Guernsey/Mail Boat/Channel Islands' and a German Hindenburg stamp cancelled with the Feldpost datestamp of 27.6.41 without number but with a small letter 'b' above the date; also a similar one from Guernsey. They are believed to have been carried on the States of Jersey steamer s.s. *Spinell* to Granville and handed over to the German Feldpost there for onward transit.

Only registered letters received the Feldpost datestamp numbered 712 (Figure 9.19) and only Germans were allowed to use the registration service. I have several examples of these letters, two of which have German stamps and two are unstamped official letters. All have the number 712 written on the registration labels.

The letters found above the date on the handstamps used in Jersey are f, g, and h.

9.19

Recently a number of Feldpost covers bearing the number 937 between 1941 and 1943 have been found in batches acquired in Germany. These also have stamps of units known to have been in the Channel Islands and it is certain that 937 was used in either Jersey or Guernsey. It is much rarer than the better known Jersey one numbered 712.

Jersey stamps are often found affixed to Feldpost letters as well as the German ones—this was entirely unnecessary and they were either affixed in ignorance or to prove the place of origin. For example, there was one gentleman who used to send off a self-addressed letter by the first local delivery to obtain the Jersey datestamp, rub out the pencilled address upon receipt, and then address the envelope to a friend in France and post it through the German Feldpost, thus having proof of the origin of the letter, the French arrival stamps, etc., proving transit.

After the Allied landings in Normandy the Feldpost in Jersey was closed for several weeks. It was re-opened on August 1, 1944, it being stated that mail would be taken to the Continent by air. When this proved to be impossible a few letters were returned to the senders, having first been marked 'Zurück' (returned) with a red handstamp.

Some of these covers known have the German Feldpost stamp of August 1, 1944, and backstamped Jersey September 26, 1944, the date they were returned.

FELDPOST STAMPS

Several German definitives of the Hitler head series are known overprinted 'Deutschefeldpost/Kanalinseln' in Gothic typeface. These may have been essays overprinted in Jersey, or they may be completely bogus. Others are known overprinted by hand in Roman characters 'Kanal-Inseln/Feld Post'. These are certainly bogus.

DIENSTPOST

A Dienstpost functioned in the Channel Islands as it did in other German-occupied territories. Its purpose was to carry correspondence of an official nature which the authorities did not wish to entrust to the Feldpost or the civilian Post Office. Covers were handstamped in violet 'Deutsche Dienstpost' and were carried by military personnel.

OFFICIAL MAIL

German soldiers were supplied with green letter sheets headed 'Feldpost', and I have one written by a soldier in Jersey to friends in Guernsey in 1943. It has no cancellations of any kind.

A letter from the German Feldkommandantur in Jersey to a local stamp dealer, giving him permission to hold an auction, has a two-line handstamp in black reading 'Feldkommandantur 515/Mil. Ver. Gr.'. A similar stamp was used in Guernsey.

Covers are known addressed to Germans in Jersey and bearing stamps cancelled with a circular handstamp with the swastika and eagle emblem in the centre and the inscription 'Dienststelle/Feldpost-nummer 40517', but these are undoubtedly philatelic.

Official mail sent by Von Helsdorf had a round handstamp reading 'Inselkommandantur Jersen' with 'Standortkommandantur' typed across it. A swastika and eagle appeared in the centre.

In 1969–70 a number of covers came from Germany with various fancy boxed cachets 'Kanalinseln', 'Luftwaffe Guernsey', 'Luftwaffe Kanalinseln', 'Kriegsmarine Jersey', and unframed 'Kanalinseln' in various sizes. Their status is doubtful.

Guernsey Mission in France

From August 16, 1940, the States of Guernsey and Jersey maintained a joint Purchasing Commission in France, with headquarters at the Villa Hirondel, Granville. The first Guernsey representatives were Messrs. R. O. Falla and W. G. Hubert and the Jersey representative Mr. John Joualt. After a few weeks Mr. Hubert was succeeded by Mr. Louis Guillemette. Mr. Falla was later replaced by Mr. P. A. Mahy, who in turn was succeeded by Mr. George Vaudin. Messrs. Vaudin and Joualt remained as the joint heads of the Purchasing Commission.

The Guernsey representative was provided with special blue envelopes bearing the two-line inscription 'ETATS DE GUERNSEY/ GRANVILLE'. One such cover, addressed to the Aerated Water Co., is stamped with a German Dienststelle handstamp in black.

It is possible that a similar envelope may have been provided for the Jersey representatives, but I have not yet seen one.

Prisoner of War and Internee Letters

Members of the British Forces found in the Channel Islands when the Germans arrived were sent to P.O.W. camps in France and Germany on July 27, 1940, and some of them tried to write to their relatives in the Islands. Two such letters may be described. One is from Bertram Morton, a P.O.W. at Cherbourg, and is addressed to his wife in Jersey. It is marked P.G. (Prisonnier de Guerre) and was posted by a French sympathizer but was marked by the French Post Office 'Inadmis/Retour a L'Envoyeur', and returned to the sender. It was then given to a Jersey fisherman who smuggled it into the island. The other, from Granville, was taken to Jersey by Joe Le Clercq, a Jersey fisherman employed by the Germans as pilot of the *Adolfe le Prince*, which ran between Jersey and Granville. It was censored by the German Naval Authorities in St. Helier, marked 'Geprüft' in red pencil and stamped in violet 'Dienststeile/Inselkommandantur/Jersey'. A message written on the back by the sender reads 'Write back Commandant Harbour Master Pilote Joe Le Clercq, Adolfe Le Prince'.

Some Channel Islands P.O.W. were interned at Stalag XXID (Posen, Poland) and Stalag IVB (Mulberg, Elbe), and covers are known from both these places.

The first deportations of Channel Island civilians took place in September, 1942. Two further groups were deported in January and February, 1943. The single men were interned at Laufen in Austria and the married couples and children at Biberach and Wurzach in Southern Germany. Some women and children were sent to Compiegne and St. Denis near Paris, with men over sixty. I can record the following items: Biberach to Guernsey, June 10, 1943; Biberach to Jersey, May 9, 1943 and February 1, 1944; Wurzach to Jersey, May 13, 1943; Laufen (Ilag VII) to Jersey, February 3, 1944; Wurzach to Jersey, February 1, 1944; St. Denis to Jersey, May 20, 1944.

Special letter cards were supplied free by the Germans to people in the Channel Islands wishing to write to their relatives in Germany.

After the liberation some Germans were kept as prisoners in the Channel Islands to dismantle the fortifications. A letter to one of them bears the Spremberg datestamp of April 29, 1946, and is addressed to Uffz. Wilhelm Baigar, B.167373, No. 802 P.O.W. Camp, Jersey, Great Britain, C.I. It is marked 'Kriegsgefangenpost' and 'Prisoner-of-War Post' and was carried free.

A Jewish concentration camp was established in Alderney in 1943 and letters are known sent from there to Paris. Full details are given in Chapter 7.

Aerial Propaganda Leaflets

On three occasions during the Occupation propaganda leaflets were dropped over the Channel Islands by the R.A.F. They are described here at Chapter 10.

Wartime Communications with Britain

Soon after the occupation of the Channel Islands by the Germans at the end of June, 1940, attempts were made by the islanders to communicate with their relatives in this country, but very few of these messages can have arrived here; there are only two known that did. The method adopted was to send such letters in a cover addressed to the British Vice-Consul in Lisbon for forwarding. One Guernseyman who had a friend interned in France wrote to him by the same means, hoping that he might be able to pass on the news to England via the Red Cross (which was not yet functioning in Guernsey). This cover, which was handed in at the German Feldpost in the Island, bore a strip of three 1d. stamps. These were not cancelled and one has been removed. As the internee died in camp it is not known if he ever received the letter, but the cover bears the censor stamp of Front-Stalag 131 at St. Lo, France, which suggests it did reach its destination. The cover was obtained from the U.S.—possibly part of some G.I.'s philatelic 'loot'.

Another cover has now been found. It bears a 3d. Postal Centenary stamp that has been left uncancelled. These Vice-Consul, Lisbon, covers were outer wrappers and contained letters to be forwarded. This second example has the name and address of the sender, a Guernsey woman, on the back. It also bears the Front-Stalag 131 censor stamp.

A method allowed to refugees in Britain wishing to communicate with their relatives in the Channel Islands was via P.O. Box 506, Lisbon, the address of Thomas Cook & Son, the official forwarding agents for mail within, to, and from enemy-occupied countries and this country. They could write letters with severely limited contents and place them in stamped envelopes and send them under cover to Thomas Cook & Son, London, together with a 2s. postal order. The

9.20 'Detained' handstamp

writers could not give any address but were to instruct their corres-
pondents to write back c/o Post Box 506, Lisbon. Several covers
sent by this service are in existence but bear a handstamp, 'Detained
in France during German Occupation.' (Figure 9.20).

From October, 1940, communication with the Islands via the Red
Cross organization was established, but at first only the name and
address of the enquirer could be transmitted. By the end of the year
a message of not more than twenty-five words was allowed. No
replies or messages from the Islands were permitted until January 13,
1941. On that date a Red Cross Bureau was opened at Elizabeth
College, Guernsey, under the supervision of George A. Bradshaw and
a staff of three, with a few voluntary helpers. The messages, which
arrived in boxes or in Red Cross sacks, were taken first of all to the

Feldkommandantur for censorship and enumeration and were then forwarded to the Bureau. The recipients were then notified by post-card and paid a visit to the Bureau to see the message and send a reply. From June, 1942, because of the large numbers of messages then arriving, the actual messages were posted to the addressees direct in special green or grey Red Cross envelopes.

For the first few months only replies to messages were dispatched and initial messages were restricted to news of births, marriages, and deaths, but from the spring of 1941 each family was allowed to send one message per month in addition to replies. An average of 10,000 monthly messages was sent from Guernsey.

In spite of the strict ban on code messages, people still managed to send scraps of information through to the mainland. Three messages in my possession conveyed a fair amount of news of local conditions. The first, dated February 14, 1942, includes the following: 'Very seldom see Senner, Sauverin, Chilcott, but see plenty of Alf's people'. Senner was a baker, Sauverin a tobacconist, and Chilcott a butcher. This meant that bread, tobacco, and meat were in very short supply. The second, dated November 14, 1942, says 'Ferguson fairly well. Seldom see Dorey. Regret Bennett Norton died 1941', meaning a fair supply of fish, little coal, and no wireless. The third, dated September 18, 1943, 'Alf's condition worsening. Family watching day and night awaiting end. Happy release'. This meant that the German position was worsening and that the islanders were waiting anxiously for liberation, which would be a happy release.

During December, 1940, Red Cross messages in small numbers began to arrive in Jersey. On January 5, 1941, 2,000 messages arrived. On March 15, 1941, the Bailiff opened an office called the Bailiff's News and Enquiry Office, and with the assistance of Mr. C. J. d'Authreau, the Assistant Postmaster, 235,744 messages were received and replied to, and 92,041 messages were sent from Jersey before communication with the mainland was cut off by the Allied invasion of France in 1944.

Three types of form were used in Great Britain. The first ones were supplied by the Comité International de la Croix Rouge at Geneva and were printed in English, French, and German. There were spaces for the names and addresses of the enquirer and the addressee and for the message. The reply was to be written on the back. In May, 1941, new forms headed 'War Organisation of the British Red Cross and Order of St. John' appeared printed in English and German only, and were addressed to the Prisoner of War, Wounded and Missing Department of the International Red Cross at Geneva. From July they were addressed instead to the Foreign Relations Department. Some forms in use in 1942–43 were again trilingual. Messages from the islands were on forms supplied by the German Red Cross in Berlin and were in French and German. Although these made similar provision on the back for a reply, none is known so used. Replies were usually sent on a fresh form and the old one retained. But all the letters I have originating in England bear replies. They mainly concern four families, two in Jersey and two in Guernsey, and it is possible to get a picture of the joy these extremely short messages brought to the recipients. They record births, illnesses, privations, and deaths, but little in a lighter vein. Through them runs an ever-present gleam of hope, poignant though it is, and just occasionally there is a brighter moment in the correspondence, as when one girl writes to her cousin: 'Hope to get engaged soon. Aubrey Green, Chester. Teacher Intermediate, second from left in school photo. Same ideas on life. Love you to meet him'. For one brief moment the war and occupation are forgotten.

During its travels each form collected a variety of handstamps, cachets, and franks, and some of these are illustrated. Let us consider the journey of one such form from England to the Channel Islands. After it had been obtained from a Red Cross Message Bureau and the twenty-five all-important words written and dated it started on its way. As a rule there was no cachet applied by the Organisation here, apart from the handstamp of the dispatching bureau, but one letter (May, 1942) bears a large double circle (56mm diameter) in red reading round the edge BRITISH RED CROSS AND ST. JOHN WAR ORGANISATION and having at the centre a 24-mm cross. Next the letters were censored and the stamp used was a vertical octagon showing a crown over PASSED and the number of the particular stamp. This was usually impressed in red, but it may also be found in grey-black, purple, and blue, and is sometimes omitted altogether.

At Geneva a small double circle reading COMITÉ INTERNATIONAL DE LA CROIX ROUGE GENÈVE was applied. At least four types were in use:

9.21

9.22

9.23

(a)   28mm diameter. Centre cross 13 × 3mm thick.

(b)   29mm diameter. Centre cross 13 × 4mm thick, and *de la* in lower-case.

(c)   32mm diameter. Cross as in (b); outer circle doubled.

(d)   36mm diameter. Otherwise as (c).

The date was then stamped at the bottom of the page and the message enclosed in a greenish-blue or grey envelope (some of which were of the window type) and forwarded to the Headquarters of the German Red Cross in France. There it received a further frank and the types used are shown.

Figure 9.21.	A 36-mm circle showing a German eagle in blue or purple with a reddish-purple cross between its feet. Used until July, 1941. Very scarce.
Figure 9.22.	*Deutsches Rotes Kreuz* in a boxed straight line in red or blue, July–December, 1941. Scarce.
Figure 9.23.	The most general type. 35-mm circle reading *Deutsches Rotes Kreuz/Der Beauftragte in Frankreich* (German Red Cross/Commissioner in France) round the edge, and *Briefstempel* (Postmark) across the middle. (The first stamp used reads *für Frankreich*). This is found in a variety of colours including red, light blue, grey-black, violet, crimson, purple, purple-brown, and bright blue between April, 1941 and April, 1944.
Figure 9.24.	As preceding, but the lettering in roman characters instead of in gothic. Seen used in October, 1943. Very scarce.
Figure 9.25.	Roman characters and now includes a conventionalized eagle and cross; the circle is enclosed in a 20-mm square. Seen in brown and red between October, 1943, and February, 1944.

This same mark was then stamped on the cover which was next forwarded to the Channel Islands.

On receipt there a card was sent to the addressee (various coloured cards are known), who was asked to call and see the communication

9.24

and to send a reply at the same time. The letter was then embossed with the seal of the Bailiff (in Jersey only) and received a cachet also.

In Jersey this read ON BEHALF OF THE BAILIFF OF JERSEY'S ENQUIRY AND NEWS SERVICE. At the very beginning this was in German round a 55-mm diameter circle (Figure 9.26), but evidently this did not find much favour in the eyes of the Jersey people and was soon replaced by three lines of rubber type in English (1941 in mauve, 1943 in blue). At the end of 1943 a proper boxed rubber handstamp was obtained. It measured 68 × 24mm and was struck in red or green.

In Guernsey the first cachet applied read 'The Controlling Committee of the States of Guernsey/Geo. A. Bradshaw/Red Cross Department'. This was soon succeeded by a boxed rubber handstamp (Figure 9.27) reading STATES OF GUERNSEY/RED CROSS BUREAU (67 × 25mm). This is known in red, violet, and green.

9.25

On its return journey to England the message collected further cachets from the German Red Cross Headquarters in France, from Geneva, and from the British Censor. Tell-tale blue streaks across the form indicate that it had been tested for secret writing.

The shortest time taken by a message in my possession was two months and the longest a year, but the average time for the journey was four months.

Two forms of particular interest are dated 1944 and 1945. The first is headed Red Cross Message Bureau and has the red cross at the left and St. John's emblem at the right. Beneath it is the legend 'Summary of Civilian Message in suspence (*sic*) at Lisbon, Portugal. Destined for the Channel Islands'. Below are three headings, FROM, DATE OF MESSAGE, MESSAGE. The form is dated 19.3.44 and is addressed to Guernsey.

The second form is a letter from the Red Cross and St. John organization at Clarence House dated May 12, 1945, which reads:

9.26   German-language marking
(*reduced*)

9.27

STATES OF GUERNSEY

RED CROSS BUREAU

Dear Sir/Madam,

We have received lists of short sentences from persons in the Channel Islands.

The following from:

Name   A. Rickett,
Address   Jersey.

is addressed to you:

'THANKS. KEEPING WELL. WALTER MIDDLING. NESSIE BEEN HOSPITAL, BETTER. LOVE.

Dated 1st March, 1945.'

Yours faithfully,

S. J. WARNER.

The Liberation

The Islands were liberated on May 9, 1945, and British forces established Field Post Offices in Guernsey and Jersey on May 12–13, which functioned until November 10. The one in Guernsey was numbered 138 and that in Jersey 302 (*see* Figures 9.28 and 9.29).

In Guernsey a circular rubber stamp with six vertical bars at top and bottom and 'ARMY/POST OFFICE' in two lines across the centre was struck in violet on small packets and parcels, the F.P.O. 138 cancellation on the back, and a registration label with 138 struck in violet after the printed 'F.P.O. No.'

As it was not known what stamps were available in the Islands special 'Post Paid' cards were made available free of charge to members of the population. They were headed 'RE-OCCUPATION OF THE CHANNEL ISLANDS' and were only allowed to be sent to addresses in the British Empire or to members of H.M. Forces. Each card bore the usual circular frank containing a crown and the words 'OFFICIAL PAID' in black. The cards were printed in England in 1944 in a quantity of 200,000.

On May 17 some letters were taken by a naval dispatch boat to Plymouth and posted on arrival. The Jersey stamps were cancelled with the Plymouth machine cancellation with the Victory Bells slogan.

The first mail sent from the Islands to Britain left on May 15.

9.28

9.29

Special commemorative covers were printed by a Guernsey stamp dealer and dated May 9. Although postmarked on the 9th they did not leave Guernsey until the 15th. Occupation stamps were used by people who still had a few left and they were valid for use from the Islands until April 13, 1946.

From the liberation the stamps were valid to all parts of the world and there are airmail covers addressed to the United States which were delivered without surcharge.

Some people tried to use the Guernsey and Jersey stamps on the mainland and in the Isle of Man. Many were accepted but others were surcharged and so the matter was referred to the Postmaster General who ruled that they were valid for use from the Islands only and not in any other part of the British Isles.

Airmail services were resumed on September 10, 1945, and commemorative covers were prepared by local dealers.

The Alderney post office, which had been closed from June 22, 1940, when the island was evacuated, was re-opened on September 21, 1945.

The Liberation Commemoratives of 1948

To commemorate the Third Anniversary of the Liberation of the Channel Islands from German Occupation, Great Britain issued on May 10, 1948, two stamps (1d. and 2½d.) depicting vraicking (seaweed gathering). The stamps were issued in Jersey, Guernsey, Alderney, and Sark and were also available at the G.P.O., London, and at Belfast, Birmingham, Bristol, Cardiff, Edinburgh, Leeds, and Manchester, remaining on sale until September 30, 1948. They were valid for postage throughout the British Isles and from many Field Post Offices abroad. (*See* Figures 9.30 and 9.31.)

9.30

9.31

The 1d. carmine was designed by J. R. R. Stobie of Harrison and Sons Ltd., and the 2½d. ultramarine by Edmund Blampied, who had previously designed the six Jersey Occupation pictorials. The stamps were printed in sheets of 120 on Multiple Crown G VI R watermarked paper by Harrison and Sons Ltd., London; perf. 15 × 14. Cylinder numbers were: 1d.—No. 2, no dot; 2½d.—No. 4, no dot. Numbers sold were: 1d.—5,934,000; 2½d.—5,398,000.

9.32   Crown flaw

9.33   Broken wheel

VARIETIES ON THE 1D. VALUE

A few sheets were found printed in a dull rose shade entirely different from the carmine of the normal and worthy of inclusion in a specialized collection. One sheet is known with a paper join running right through the top row of stamps making a double thickness and causing the doctor blade to jam and leave a heavy red line right across the top stamps; row 5 shows an irregular white line running right across the sheet giving the impression of a cracked cylinder.

VARIETIES ON THE 2½D. VALUE

Two constant varieties can be found on the 2½d. 'The defective crown' (Figure 9.32) occurs on the first stamp in the sheet and has the left arm of the centre cross elongated downwards into the base of the crown, causing a break in the blue line of pearls above the centre jewels. 'The broken wheel,' which appears on the fifth stamp in the bottom row, shows a white patch of irregular shape on the wheels (Figure 9.33).

10

AIR SERVICES

Airmails

A French seaplane base was established in Guernsey at the southern end of St. Peter Port harbour in July, 1917. Huts were erected by the Royal Navy and a Bessonau shed was sent from France.

The base was under the command of Lieut. de Vaisseau Le Cour Grandmaison. There were three pilots (Lambert, Bourgault, and Sylvestre) of whom one was an officer, and three observers (Rolin, Parmentier, and Boissand). It was intended to have twelve seaplanes at the base but only two were sent in July. In September it was decided that the strength of the base be raised to sixteen patrol aircraft.

Bad weather in the winter caused real difficulties. On December 19, 1917, the motor launch was lost. The commander of the Normandy squadrons was unable to supply the torpedo boat that the base needed. The position was bad for take-off and landing and, because of the winds, the roofs of the portable hangers were in a very bad state. In view of this the Commandant recommended that the base be transferred to Cherbourg.

In January, 1918, the strength of the base was eleven Telliers and ten F.B.A.s. In February and March activity was much reduced because of damage to the crane.

Enseigne de Vaisseau Flandrin replaced Lieut. Le Cour de Grandmaison as commanding officer of the base.

The seaplane base remained in Guernsey until December, 1918, when the aircraft were flown to Cherbourg and the 150 men attached to the base left the island.

Two cachets were used on mail sent from the base, which was

10.1 Cachet of French seaplane base

carried to Cherbourg by seaplanes of the squadron and posted there. The first cachet is circular and is inscribed 'Service a la Mer 2D' and CENTRE D'AVION/MARITIME/de GUERNESEY. This is on a card dated December 1, 1917, bearing Christmas greetings. The second cachet has an anchor in the centre and ESCADRILLE D'AVIATION MARITIME DE GUERNESEY in a double circle (Figure 10.1). This is known struck in blue on several cards from members of the squadron and on a cover addressed to Croydon bearing a British stamp.

It is interesting to note that L. V. Lambert, one of the pilots, became French Consul in Guernsey many years later.

SOUTHAMPTON–GUERNSEY FLIGHT, 1919

The earliest recorded flight from England to the Channel Islands was on October 5, 1919, during the Railway Strike period, when an unsuccessful attempt was made to carry *Lloyds Weekly News* from Southampton to Guernsey, the pilot of the machine being compelled to alight on the sea near Alderney. Papers were imprinted 'By Seaplane, Special Edition,' and after the accident were overprinted with a message from the pilot apologizing for his failure.

EXPERIMENTAL FLIGHT, 1935

In an effort to demonstrate to the Postal Authorities how great a saving of time could be effected by carrying mail by air to the Channel Islands, Whoopee Sports Ltd. had a small quantity of covers (less than 100) addressed to Roborough Aerodrome, Plymouth, and posted locally at 5 a.m. on Friday, June 27, 1935. These were flown to Jersey at noon and arrived at 1.15 p.m., landing on the beach. The letters were then re-stamped and re-addressed with a grey label covering the old address and were re-posted in Jersey receiving the 4.15 p.m. cancellation on the same day. The service, however, proved unsuitable for mail-carrying purposes, due to the non-existence of an aerodrome and the fact that the time-table varied with the tides.

OFFICIAL FLIGHT, 1937

An aerodrome was constructed in Jersey in 1937 and a contract for the transport of first-class mail was awarded to Jersey Airways, the first flights taking place on June 1. The plane from Jersey left at 6.25 a.m. and arrived at Southampton at 7.37 a.m. with 335 lb of mail. That from Southampton left at 7.50 a.m., arriving at Jersey at 8.50 a.m. with 229 lb of mail.

An angular cachet reading JERSEY AIRWAYS LTD/FIRST/AIR/MAIL/FLIGHT/1st JUNE/1937 (Figure 10.2) was applied to covers handled at the Company's offices in London, Jersey or Southampton. Each office used a distinctive coloured ink as follows: London—green, Jersey—blue, Southampton—violet. A similar cachet struck in red was used by a well-known dealer, A. Phillips, on letters from New-

10.2 (approx. three-quarters actual size)

JERSEY AIRWAYS LTD
—o—
FIRST
AIR
MAIL
FLIGHT
—o—
1ST JUNE
1937
—o—

port, Mon. The Jersey and Southampton covers were also endorsed 'FROM JERSEY' or 'FROM SOUTHAMPTON' in the same coloured ink as the cachet.

Covers with meter stamps of Jersey Airways are scarcer than those with adhesives. The slogan attached to the Jersey Airways meter stamp read 'JERSEY (emblem) AIRWAYS/VICTORIA RLY STATION PHONE VICTORIA 5692/5/1$\frac{1}{2}$ HRS——LONDON—FARE £5/OR FROM/EXETER–SOUTHAMPTON–BRIGHTON'. After the £5 the letters 'RTN' are inserted vertically in tiny type.

GUERNSEY FLIGHTS, 1939

(a)

(b)

10.3 (approx. three-quarters actual size)

The Southampton–Guernsey service by Guernsey Airways Ltd. commenced on May 8, 1939, a plane leaving Southampton at 8 a.m. and arriving at Guernsey at 8.59 a.m. Flown covers usually bear the 11.45 p.m. postmark of Southampton dated May 7, 1939. Some covers received the cachets shown in Figures 10.3(a) and (b), the rectangular cachet usually being struck in purple and the circular in green. The aircraft was RMA G–ACZP and the pilot B. Walker.

The first flight from Guernsey took place on May 22, 1939. The plane left Guernsey at 6.28 a.m. and arrived at Southampton at 7.25 a.m. The pilot was J. B. W. Pugh. The usual postmark seen on flown covers is St. Peter Port, Guernsey, 5 a.m. May 22, 1939. Covers have been seen bearing both cachets (Figures 10.3(a) and (b)) with the dates altered, struck very faintly in black. Privately printed souvenir covers of several kinds exist.

JERSEY–GUERNSEY FLIGHT, 1939

Also on May 22, mail was flown for the first time from Jersey to Guernsey, the plane leaving Jersey at 6 a.m. and arriving at Guernsey 15 minutes later. No special cachets were applied and genuine flown covers are very rare. They normally bear the 5 a.m. Jersey postmark of May 22, 1939. The aircraft was RMA G–ADVK and the pilot J. B. W. Pugh.

The return flight from Guernsey to Jersey did not take place until July 10, 1939. Details of time of departure, etc., are not known. Very little mail was carried owing to inadequate notice being given of the institution of the service. The usual postmark is that of Guernsey timed 5 a.m. on July 10, 1939. Regular services continued until war was declared on September 3, 1939, when all air services between Southampton and the Islands ceased.

SHOREHAM–CHANNEL ISLANDS SERVICE, 1939

A service between Shoreham and the Islands was resumed on November 8, 1939, running to Jersey and Guernsey on Mondays, Wednesdays, and Fridays, and from the Islands on Tuesdays, Thursdays, and Saturdays. Daily services operated from December 11, until the German Occupation on July 1, 1940, when all services were suspended.

RESUMPTION OF AIR SERVICES, 1945

On September 10, 1945, air services between Southampton and Jersey and Guernsey were resumed in both directions, and also the inter–island services. Special souvenir covers were prepared and were flown from Southampton at 6.30 a.m., Jersey at 9.20 a.m., and

10.6 First air flight after Liberation. Note scarce Parcel Depot cancellation

10.4

10.5

Guernsey at 10.05 a.m. Some covers received a circular cachet (Figure 10.4) in purple applied in Jersey, or a rectangular one (Figure 10.5) in blue applied in Guernsey. Covers sent from Guernsey to Jersey also received the rare GUERNSEY CH. IS. PARCEL DEPOT cancellation dated 10 SP 45 (Figure 10.6).

GUERNSEY–ALDERNEY SERVICE, 1946

The first flight from Guernsey to Alderney took place on June 18, 1946, and the return flight was made on the same day. No special markings were applied to letters flown, of which there were eleven from Guernsey to Alderney and forty from Alderney to Guernsey, but they were initialled by the Sub-Postmaster and back-stamped with the Alderney datestamp.

B.E.A. TAKE-OVER, 1947

When the airlines were nationalized in 1947 the Channel Islands services were taken over by British European Airways and the rectangular datestamps of the Jersey, Guernsey, and Southampton offices were applied to letters carried on some flights under the new regime from April 1. The Jersey stamp was in violet and was lettered A at the bottom; the Guernsey stamp was in violet and was lettered T at the bottom; and the Southampton one was in red and was lettered A at the bottom. Last-day covers under the old service on March 31 have a circular cachet of Channel Islands Airways. This was the parent company of both Jersey and Guernsey Airways and was formed in 1934.

FIRST ALDERNEY–SOUTHAMPTON DIRECT MAIL, 1947

On May 20, 1947, a direct flight was made from Alderney to Southampton and twelve letters were carried by arrangement with the pilot and the Sub-Postmaster of Alderney. They were autographed by the pilot and posted on arrival at Southampton.

SCOTTISH AIRLINES FLIGHT, 1952

Scottish Airlines inaugurated a regular passenger service between

Prestwick and Jersey in the summer of 1952, and on the first flight on June 14, 1952, the pilot, Captain J. C. Grant, carried seven letters which were posted on arrival in Jersey. The covers were stamped in four lines in violet SCOTTISH AIRLINES/PRESTWICK JERSEY/FIRST FLIGHT/ 14 JUN 1952 and were signed by the pilot.

B.E.A. AIRWAY LETTER SERVICES, 1953

On October 20, 1953, British European Airways extended their Airways Letter Service to the Channel Islands, using the then current B.E.A. stamps for prepayment of their charges. The rates charged were 7d. for letters up to 2 oz, 1s. from 2 oz to 4 oz, and 1s. 6d. from 4 oz to 1 lb, in addition to the ordinary inland postage. Letters had to be properly stamped and handed in to the B.E.A. office or airport endorsed 'To be called for' or 'To be posted on arrival.' The letters were then flown to their destination and those marked 'To be posted on arrival' were dropped into the nearest pillar box and the postage stamps were cancelled by the Post Office. A letter from London to Jersey would have the B.E.A. stamp cancelled in London and the postage stamp cancelled on arrival in Jersey. If marked 'To be called for' the postage stamp would be cancelled in Jersey by B.E.A., either with the rectangular datestamp of the local office, with a rubber stamp reading CANCELLED, or by pen. The flights were made between Jersey and London, Guernsey and London, Jersey and Guernsey, and Guernsey and Alderney.

10.7

Increased Rates, 1953–57

On November 25, 1953, the B.E.A. rates were raised to 8d., 1s. 2d., and 1s. 9d. and new stamps were issued (Figure 10.7).

The rates were raised to 9d., 1s. 3d., and 1s. 11d. on September 1, 1954, using stamps of the same design with the values printed in black instead of in the colour of the stamps.

On June 27, 1956, the rates were increased to 10d., 1s. 5d., and 2s. 2d. and new stamps of smaller format were issued (Figure 10.8). When the rates were raised again on July 1, 1957, to 11d., 1s. 6d., and 2s. 4d., stamps of the same design were used.

The reason for the almost annual increases in rates was the increased railway freight charges. The charge for airway letters must be the

10.8

same as that for railway letters and when British Rail put their charges up the Postmaster General insisted that British European Airways do the same.

Only during the 1953 and 1954 rate increases were first day covers flown between London and Guernsey and London and Jersey, although, of course, genuine commercial covers can be found flown on later dates.

Embargo on Flights from Channel Islands to London

Because of difficulties with H.M. Customs at London Airport, British European Airways were forced to suspend their Airway Letter Service to London from Jersey and Guernsey from July 24 to September 2, 1956, and then discontinue it altogether. There has been no embargo on the carriage of letters *to* the Islands from Britain. Some covers handed in at Guernsey on July 24 were marked 'Received before embargo' and were carried in the normal way.

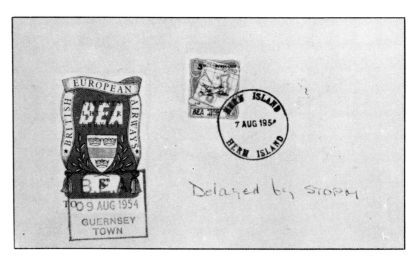

10.9 'Delayed by storm' endorsement

Herm Feeder Service, 1954

To connect up with the B.E.A. Service from Guernsey, the tenant of Herm issued on August 7, 1954, a special 5d. stamp to prepay carriage on letters from Herm to the B.E.A. office in Guernsey. This took the form of the current 2d. definitive overprinted '3d. SUR-CHARGE B.E.A. AIRWAY LETTER SERVICE'. First-day covers were cancelled on August 7 but because of a storm they were not taken over to Guernsey until August 9. They were endorsed in manuscript 'Delayed by storm' (Figure 10.9). A few covers posted on September 1, 1954, the first day of the increased B.E.A. rates, had the obsolete B.E.A. 8d. stamp affixed instead of the 9d., but they were allowed to pass. This was the only occasion on which insufficiently stamped letters were carried by B.E.A.

Increased Rates, 1961–71

The rate was increased from 11d. to 1s. on October 4, 1961, and 100 covers were flown from London to Jersey. They bear the datestamps of the Air Mail Branch, London, and Jersey Airport.

A new series of Airway Letter stamps was issued in 1964 and covers bearing the 1s. stamp were flown from London to Jersey on May 27.

A further series was issued in 1970 and letters bearing the 3s. 7d. stamp were flown from London to Guernsey on May 1. On February 15, 1971, covers with decimal 18p., 21p., and 26p. were flown to Guernsey and Jersey.

FREEDOM GROUP POST, 1964

During a postal worker's work-to-rule in January, 1964, the Freedom Group, an organization run by Mr. Edward Martell in London, carried parcels by air to various parts of the United Kingdom. Only one parcel was carried to Jersey on January 17 franked by two 5s. and a 6d. Freedom Group stamps.

CAMBRIAN AIRWAYS FLIGHT, 1964

On December 2, 1964, Cambrian Airways carried letters from Bristol to Guernsey and from Guernsey to Jersey. Special 1s. Cambrian Airways Air Letter stamps were used.

HELICOPTER FLIGHT, 1965

On November 1, 1965, B.E.A. carried 100 covers from Jersey to Guernsey and 100 covers from Guernsey to Jersey by helicopter. They carried 1s. B.E.A. Airway Letter stamps cancelled at the airports. The covers from Jersey had a black rectangular cachet featuring a helicopter and inscribed FIRST SCHEDULED HELICOPTER FLIGHT JERSEY/ GUERNSEY. The covers from Guernsey had a similar cachet in green inscribed GUERNSEY/JERSEY.

BRITISH UNITED FLIGHT, 1966

On August 5, 1966, British United Airways carried a dozen covers from Paris to Jersey. They were franked by French 60c. stamps and carried a red boxed cachet reading BRITISH UNITED/PARIS JERSEY/5 Aout 1966. On arrival in Jersey they received the British United datestamp of Jersey Airport.

30TH ANNIVERSARY OF FIRST AIRMAIL, 1969

To commemorate the thirtieth anniversary of the first airmail from Guernsey to England, special covers were flown on May 22 by L. E. Batchelor in a Cessna 172. The aircraft first called at Jersey to carry mail from Jersey to Guernsey and there picked up mail for England. The flight terminated at Thruxton. There were 150 matched pairs of covers signed by the pilot and a further 350 unsigned covers. A few of the original 1939 covers were also re-flown.

INAUGURATION OF NEW POSTAL ADMINISTRATIONS, 1969

To commemorate the inauguration of the new Jersey and Guernsey Postal Administrations, British European Airways carried 1,000 covers from each island to Heathrow. Both covers carry the B.E.A. insignia and the inscription '1st October, 1969 British European Airways Commemorate the Inauguration of the States of Jersey (Guernsey) Postal Administration'.

The Jersey covers bear the Jersey 2s. 6d. stamp featuring the airport and cancelled with the special Jersey first-day postmark. They also have the boxed B.E.A. Jersey Airport datestamp of October 1, 1969.

The Guernsey covers have the Guernsey ½d., 1d., 1½d., and 5d. stamps cancelled with the special day of issue postmark. They carry no B.E.A. markings.

AURIGNY AIRWAYS FLIGHTS, 1970

On November 16, 1970, Aurigny Air Services made inaugural flights from Alderney to Cherbourg and return. Special covers were prepared by Picton Publishing of Chippenham, Wilts., and marketed by Rushstamps of Southampton and Georges Robbé of Jersey. The covers carried normal Guernsey and French stamps, but had Aurigny Air Services cachets.

GUERNSEY−ALDERNEY FLIGHT, 1970

To commemorate the twenty-fifth anniversary of the islanders' return to Alderney after World War II special covers were flown by Aurigny Air Services from Guernsey to Alderney on December 2, 1970.

JERSEY−PARIS FLIGHT BY B.I.A., 1971

To mark the opening of the air service from Jersey to Paris (Orly) a special cover was produced by Crown Philatelic Productions with a frontal sketch of a Handley Page Dart Herald in flight and a map of Jersey and France in black and olive. The cover carries the boxed datestamp of the British Island Airways Administration, Jersey Airport, of January 24 and the arrow symbol of BIA and the back-stamp of BIA Orly Aerogare.

JERSEY−MANCHESTER FLIGHT, 1971

A special cover was produced by Crown Philatelic Productions for the first flight from Jersey to Manchester by BIA on April 3, 1971. It depicts a Handley Page Dart Herald and a map of the route and carries the boxed datestamp of BIA Jersey Airport of April 3, 1971, and the arrival stamp of Servisair, Manchester Airport, of April 3, 1971. The cover also carries a handstamp giving the flight details.

149

JERSEY–STAVERTON FLIGHT, 1971

Also on April 3 Intra Airways Ltd. made a special flight to Staverton and return and Crown Philatelic Productions produced special covers for the occasion. These were cacheted by Intra Airways at Jersey and Cheltenham and carry handstamp flight details.

JERSEY–BREST FLIGHT, 1971

Rousseau Aviation made a flight to Brest on June 12, 1971, and a special cover was produced by Crown Philatelic Productions. It carries a rubber handstamp in blue giving the flight details.

GUERNSEY–CHERBOURG FLIGHT, 1971

On June 12 (postponed from June 5), 1971, Rousseau Aviation made a special flight from Guernsey to Cherbourg. A pictorial cover was produced by Crown Philatelic Productions and carried a black rubber handstamp giving the flight details.

ALDERNEY–GUERNSEY ANNIVERSARY FLIGHT, 1971

To mark the 25th anniversary of the first airmail from Alderney to Guernsey a special flight was made from Alderney to Guernsey and return by Aurigny Air Services on June 18, 1971. Special pictorial covers were produced by Crown Philatelic Productions.

JERSEY–LE HAVRE FLIGHT, 1971

Rousseau Aviation made a special flight from Jersey to Le Havre on July 3, 1971. Covers prepared by Crown Philatelic Productions were flown and were cacheted with details of the flight and the datestamps of Jersey and Le Havre airports.

Hovercraft Mail

A series of Hovercraft Flights was made in January and February, 1971. On January 4 a flight was made from Gosport, Hants, to St. Helier by Hovercraft VT1–001 by Captain B. Goldsmith. The return flight was made on February 4 and because of the British postal strike a 3s. black on green local stamp was produced featuring the hovercraft and inscribed FIRST FLIGHT/JERSEY TO GOSPORT/3/-.

On January 6 a flight was made from Jersey to Guernsey and return, and on January 7 a flight was made to Dinard and return. Special pictorial covers were produced by Crown Philatelic Productions and the covers were all cacheted by rubber handstamp giving details of the flights.

Aerial Propaganda Leaflets

During World War II Allied propaganda leaflets were dropped over every occupied country. The Channel Islands were not forgotten and examples of those dropped there make interesting reading and are keenly sought after by collectors of Channel Islands stamps and postal history material.

Two classes of leaflet were dropped, the first in English for the information and comfort of the civilian population and the second in German for the demoralization of the occupying forces.

LEAFLETS FOR CIVILIANS

In the first group are four leaflets but only three were actually dropped. The first (Figure 10.10) is headed 'News from England' in gothic letters, and is dated September, 1940. It is inscribed 'Distributed by the R.A.F.', and has as its main feature a message from His Majesty The King. It is numbered 600/1 and was dropped on the night of 23/24 September, 1940.

The second is somewhat similar but bears the inscription 'News from England' in roman letters and is dated September 30, 1940. It is also inscribed 'Distributed by the R.A.F.' and 'For the Channel Islands.' It is numbered 600/2 and was dropped between 7/8 and 15/16 October, 1940.

The third leaflet is a rather attractive one entitled 'The Archbishop of York speaks to the people of the Channel Islands' and is printed in red and black. Its four pages contain the sermon preached by the Archbishop on Sunday, January 31, 1943, at 9.30 a.m. in St. Martin-in-the-Fields Church, and broadcast in the B.B.C. Home Service.

News from England

No. 1   SEPTEMBER 1940   DISTRIBUTED BY THE R.A.F.

To The Channel-Islanders

All of you, His Majesty's loyal subjects on the Channel Islands, must keep asking yourselves two great questions :—" How long must we put up with the German occupation ? " and " How are our friends on the mainland ? "

This news-sheet brings you the heartening answers. We on the mainland are in good heart. By subjecting our women and children to the wickedest form of warfare known to history, Hitler has only stiffened our backs. And the events of the last three weeks have only served to confirm Mr. Churchill's words of August 21st, that " the road to victory may not be so long as we expect." Nor may the day be so distant when we shall come to your relief. All our rapidly and enormously increasing strength is directed towards that day when the shadow of the bully will be lifted from you and from the whole of Europe. We shall continue to bring you the news from England as often and as regularly as we can.

A MESSAGE FROM HIS MAJESTY THE KING

The Queen and I desire to convey to you our heartfelt sympathy in the trials which you are now enduring. We earnestly pray for your speedy liberation, knowing that it will surely come.

GEORGE R. I.

Bombs over Germany

Hitler has suffered his first major defeat. While the mass raids on Britain have been broken up at a devastating cost to the Luftwaffe, the Royal Air Force carries out nightly raids on Germany and the Occupied Territories with such precision and intensity that the Hitler war machine has been visibly weakened.

The attacks on Germany have now lasted three months. From the North Sea to the borders of Czechoslovakia, from the Baltic to the Swiss Frontier, there is no military objective which is safe from them. Across the Alps, too, heavy blows have been struck at such targets in Milan, Turin, Genoa and other industrial centres.

Only military targets are attacked, but the effect has been that much the more serious. It contrasts strikingly with the indiscriminate terror bombing over England carried out by pilots who lack the training for more damaging tactics.

In Berlin itself gasworks, power stations, armament factories and railway stations have been repeatedly and systematically bombed. Hamm, key terminus for Ruhr rail traffic, has been bombed over sixty times. The Dortmund-Ems Canal, another vital artery, has been pierced by the heaviest bombs and drained.

At Hamburg and Emden vast areas of the docks have been wiped out. Synthetic petrol installations at Stettin and Leuna, reservoirs at Kiel, power stations at Nuremberg and Munich have all felt the weight of the British fist.

The great German forests have been set on fire. In the Black Forest, the Harz and the forest of Thuringia outside Berlin, walls of flame have closed around hidden factories and munition stores until explosions broke out.

Besides these blows at the heart of Germany, the fortified ports in Norway, Holland, Belgium and France, where the Germans are concentrating for the suicidal attempt at invasion, have been repeatedly struck.

In Africa and Italian possessions in the Mediterranean a similar story has been written by the R.A.F. with the difference that the Italian anti-aircraft defences and fighting planes are weaker than the German.

UP AND UP

" Our production of aircraft already largely exceeds the enemy's." This important announcement was made by Mr. Winston Churchill on August 20th. " The American production is only just beginning to flow in," he added. " Our fighter and bomber strengths are now, after all this fighting, larger than they have ever been."

The Luftwaffe was then attempting to put our aircraft industry out of action. It was in vain. At the end of the month Lord Beaverbrook, Minister of Aircraft Production, was able to add his own statement to the Prime Minister's. He said :

" The men and women of the aircraft industry of Great Britain have provided for the R.A.F. in the last week more fighters and bombers than ever before in the history of aviation ".

A World against Germany

Large numbers of the new bombers shattering Germany and of the fighters defending our coasts will bear the names of cities thousands of miles away from Europe. Gifts have poured in from every continent.

A bomber and three fighters from British Guiana ; two Hurricanes from the Bahamas ; three hundred Spitfires from Ceylon ; fifty Spitfires from the Gold Coast ; seventy-five more from Hyderabad ; eighty more from East India ; twelve bombers from Malaya ; a bomber and two fighters from Mauritius ; two Spitfires from Mombasa ; £100,000 from New Zealand to be spent at Lord Beaverbrook's discretion ; ten Spitfires from Sarawak (and one from the Rajah) ; three bombers from Trinidad ; one Spitfire from St. Vincent and another from Granada in the Windward Isles ; four Spitfires from Zanzibar ; more fighters and bombers from Uganda ; more again from Rhodesia and a promise of regular monthly supplies ; more again still from Southern Rhodesia ; Spitfires yet again from the " Speed the Planes " fund in Natal ; large consignments of rupees from Madras.

All over the British Isles, meanwhile, individuals,

groups of employees, towns and suburbs have presented Spitfires and Hurricanes to the nation. Every kind of group has subscribed, money has even come from people bearing the same christian name—the Harolds, the Georges, etc.

From everywhere come fighters and bombers, bombers and fighters, most of all Squadrons of Spitfires.

By courtesy of 'The Evening Standard'

IMPREGNABLE TARGET

Free France Rises Anew

Throughout the French Empire and in France itself there are signs that the spirit of France, which was temporarily numbed by the shock of defeat, is now re-awakening.

Immediately after the capitulation, General de Gaulle raised in England the banner of les Français libres. Then, on August 26th, all the French possessions in Central West Africa—the Chad, the French Cameroons, the French Congo and Oubangui-Chari—suddenly and with one accord rallied to the cause of Free France.

In those French possessions which are still under the domination of the Axis, there are signs of revolt. An unascertainable number of fighting planes from French Morocco have arrived at Gibraltar, piloted by French airmen who wish to fight with General de Gaulle. The French naval forces in the Mediterranean and at Djibuti are reported to be eagerly waiting for the moment when they can re-enter the war.

In France itself, where the Nazi boot presses most heavily, there are also signs of resurrection. The Vichy government has rejected the demand, presented by the Germans, for more than half the livestock in unoccupied France. The Germans, as they naturally tend to do, are over-reaching themselves in their greed and are provoking growing resistance. There is evidence of sabotage in the factories now working for Germany. The broadcasts of General de Gaulle are eagerly listened to, despite German threats of severe punishment. The time is not far off when in France, too, the revolt, which is still underground, will flame up into the open.

ON THE REBOUND

By courtesy of 'The Star'

6:0

He took as his text the famous words from Isaiah 'Comfort ye, comfort ye my people, saith your God.' The leaflet also has pictures of the Archbishop and of St. Martin-in-the-Fields. It is numbered J1 and was dropped on 4/5 March, 1943.

The fourth leaflet, which for some reason was never dropped, bears on one side the Royal Arms and in bold capitals 'To the inhabitants of the Channel Islands'; and on the other is a statement made in the House of Commons by the Home Secretary, Mr. Herbert Morrison, on Tuesday, December 12, 1944. The statement deals with the sending of medicine, soap, and food parcels to the Islanders. The leaflet is numbered J2.

LEAFLETS FOR OCCUPATION FORCES

The second group of leaflets consists of a series of over 300 prepared by S.H.A.E.F. (Supreme Headquarters Allied Expeditionary Forces) and dropped almost daily, by the British and American Forces, behind the enemy front line and over isolated garrisons in the Channel Islands and elsewhere. They are the famous *Nachrichten* newspapers and gave the German forces latest details of the Allied war effort. Not every one of the series was dropped over the Channel Islands, and it is in any case virtually impossible to obtain the whole lot, so those interested are advised to include a representative selection, particularly the issues of April–August, 1944, many of which were definitely disseminated on the Islands. The leaflets are numbered from T9 to T381.

One issue of the famous *Le Courrier de L'Air* series, which was dropped regularly over France, was actually dropped in Jersey. This was the issue for March 23, 1944.

A miniature German newspaper, *Front und Heimat* (Front and Home), was dropped over the Channel Islands by the Luftwaffe for the German Forces after they were cut off from France by the Allies.

A 12-page, sepia-coloured, illustrated booklet in English headed 'We Protest', and with a picture of Field-Marshal Montgomery on the front, was distributed in Jersey by the Germans one night in 1944 after the Allied landings in Normandy. It purported to be a leaflet prepared by Allied soldiers, protesting at the politicians' presentation of the German soldier as a weakling. The text is rather crude and contains one or two obscene words.

Included in the disseminations for the German troops by the Allies were certain items of 'black' propaganda, i.e. purporting to come from enemy sources. No details of these have been given officially, but known to have been dropped on the Channel Islands are certain small booklets, having the appearance of genuine German stories but including a great deal of information, with illustrations, upon how to 'go sick' and deceive the German Medical Officers so as to avoid fighting. It is interesting to note that similar information was dropped in English by the Germans upon our troops in Italy, and it would seem probable that much of the information was copied from these Allied booklets!

Other Material

There are other rare and interesting items which can be included in a collection of Channel Islands airmails.

In 1870 during the Siege of Paris in the Franco-Prussian War letters were flown out of Paris by balloon and a number of them exist addressed to the Channel Islands. I have several that have been flown out of Paris and then carried by sea to Jersey. They are the *ballons montés*, of which I have examples carried by *Le Victor Hugo*, on October 18, with Jersey backstamp of October 22, 1870; *Le Parmentier* on December 17, 1870, with Jersey backstamp of January 1, 1871; *Le Gambetta* on January 10, 1871; *La Poste de Paris* on January 18, 1871. The latter is a copy of the *Gazette des Absents*. Others known are *La Bataille de Paris* of December 1, 1870, *La Ville de Florence* of September 25, 1870, and *Le Duquesne* of January 9, 1871, in the collection of Monsieur Pierre Langlois of Paris. The letter carried by *La Bataille de Paris* is a copy of the *Gazette des Absents* and that carried by *Le Duquesne* has been re-addressed to Jersey from Dover and bears the backstamps of Dover, London and Jersey. A number of other *ballons montés* are in collections of members of the Channel Islands Specialists' Society.

I have also a letter from Jersey to Paris endorsed 'Par Ballon' which was sent to Lille for an attempted flight into Paris. The flight was unsuccessful and the letter was delivered in Paris on February 25,

1871, after the Siege had been lifted. Monsieur Langlois has similar covers.

In 1911 the London to Windsor Coronation Aerial Flights were made and some of the letters and postcards were addressed to the Channel Islands. I have several addressed to Jersey and backstamped on arrival.

11

THE REGIONAL STAMPS

In July, 1956, the Postmaster General announced that the Queen had agreed in principle to the issue of regional stamps for Britain and that Jersey and Guernsey were each to have a 2½d. stamp. Shortly afterwards advisory committees were formed to advise the Postmaster General on the choice of subjects and artists for the new stamps. Designs (eight in Guernsey and several in Jersey) were submitted anonymously to the committees and from them the final selection was made.

In Guernsey a design by Eric Piprell, a Guernseyman, was chosen. It shows the Crown of William the Conqueror from the second silver penny of William I and the Guernsey lily as described in the book *The Lilium Sarniense*, by James Douglas, published in 1725. Before the stamp was ready postage rates had increased and the denomination was changed to 3d., the normal letter rate, otherwise the stamp would have been in almost the same colour as the Guernsey lily.

The Jersey stamp was designed by William M. Gardner, who chose the Mace presented to the island by Charles II in 1663, and the Arms of Jersey as his main subjects, with potato and tomato plant in the borders to emphasize the importance of the agricultural produce of the island.

Both stamps were photogravure-printed by Harrison and Sons Ltd., High Wycombe, in sheets of 240 from single cylinders. They are on paper watermarked multiple St. Edward's Crown, perforated 15 × 14. The colour of both stamps is pale violet.

The stamps were issued on August 18, 1958.

A 2½d. was added for each island on June 8, 1964 for use on tourists' postcards. To save going back to the design committees it was

11.1 Edmund Blampied's rough sketch for Jersey
2½d., not accepted for first issue (3d.) but revived
when a 2½d. was required in 1964

decided to use the second-choice designs in the original competition. The Guernsey design was by Eric Piprell and featured a variation of the Lily and Crown theme. The Jersey design was by Edmund Blampied and featured the Arms and the Mace (Figure 11.1). One sheet of the Jersey stamp had the bottom row of stamps imperforate.

New 4d. denominations in blue, for the increased letter rate, were issued on February 7, 1966, in the designs of the 3d. stamps. In 1967 the 3d. and 4d. were both issued with phosphor lines.

When the two-tier letter post was introduced in September, 1968, the colour of the 4d. stamps, for second-class mail, was changed to sepia and 5d. values were issued in Stuart blue for the first-class rate on the fourth of the month. The colour of the 4d. was changed to red on February 26, 1969, because of confusion between the 4d. and 5d. colours under artificial light. These three values were on un-watermarked paper with PVA gum.

The Regional stamps were withdrawn from sale in Guernsey and Jersey on September 30, 1969, when the Islands established their own postal services. They continued to be accepted for postal use in Jersey until October 31, 1969, and in Guernsey until about the end of March, 1970, following representations of the Guernsey Hoteliers Association.

The stamps continued to be valid in the United Kingdom although they were withdrawn from sale at the Philatelic Bureau and Counters on September 30, 1970, finally being invalidated in February, 1972.

A full list of the denominations, varieties, errors, and flaws follows. The description R12/8, etc., refers to the position of a variety on the sheet, e.g. Row 12 stamp No. 8. [Catalogue numbers are from the *Specialised Priced Catalogue of Channel Islands Stamps*.]

Guernsey

1958-69. Designed by Eric Piprell. Photo. Harrison & Sons Ltd. in sheets of 240 (12 × 20). Watermark Multiple Crown. Perforated 15 × 14 comb. Figure 11.2.

28. 2½d. rose-red (June 8, 1964)
    a.   deep rose-red (Cyl. 3, 1964)
29. 3d. deep lilac (August 18, 1958)
    a.   whiter paper (July 5, 1962)
    b.   pale lilac (April, 1967)
30. 4d. deep blue (February 7, 1966)
    a.   spur on stem to lily (R12/8)

               Watermark as above. Phosphor lines.
31. 3d. pale lilac (May 24, 1967)
32. 4d. deep blue (October 24, 1967)
    a.   spur on stem to lily (R12/8)

11.2   Guernsey regionals

No watermark. Chalky paper. Phosphor lines. PVA gum.

33. 4d. deep blue (April 16, 1968)
    a.   missing phosphor
    b.   spur on stem to lily (R12/8)
34. 4d. sepia (September 4, 1968)
    a.   missing phosphor
    b.   phosphor horizontal
    c.   spur on stem to lily (R12/8)
    d.   damaged '4' of 4d. (R16/10)
35. 4d. red (February 26, 1969)
    a.   stem flaw retouched
36. 5d. Stuart blue (September 4, 1968)
    a.   deep Stuart blue (August, 1969)
    b.   large spot on centre stamen of lily (R12/1)
    c.   retouched spot (R12/1)

CYLINDER NUMBERS (all no dot)

2½d.	No. 1	4d. blue (no wmk.), No. 1	
2½d.	No. 3	a. missing phosphor	
3d.	No. 4	4d. sepia No. 1	
3d.	No. 5	a. missing phosphor	
3d. (phos.)	No. 5	4d. red No. 1	
4d. blue	No. 1	5d. blue No. 1	
4d. (phos.)	No. 1		

11.3 Jersey regionals

Jersey

1958–69. Designed by W. M. Gardner. Photo. Harrison & Sons Ltd. in sheets of 240 (12 × 20). Watermark Multiple Crown. Perforated 15 × 14 comb. Figure 11.3.

34. 2½d. carmine-red (June 8, 1964)
    a.   imperf. three sides (vert. pair)
    b.   part imperf.
    c.   thin letters (R18/1)

One sheet of the 2½d. was found in St. Helier with the bottom row imperforate on three sides. This was split into pairs and blocks of four and one pair is known used on cover. Another sheet was found with the lower right corner folded over before perforating, leaving the last stamp on the sheet imperforate on two sides.

35. 3d. deep lilac (August 18, 1958)
    a.   'halberd' flaw—large white flaw joining leaf to mace (R20/3)
    b.   retouched
    c.   tomato on truss at left joined to leaf below (R19/9)
    d.   retouch
    e.   white flaw on small tomato leaf above truss at left of plant (R1/5)
    f.   white flaw on right of top leaf of potato plant (R1/6)
    g.   extra tomato in truss on left of plant (R9/1)
    h.   white flaw below third leaf on left of tomato plant (R10/3)
    i.   tail to 'D' (R20/3)
    j.   with perforated initials of A. de Gruchy
    k.   white paper (September 23, 1962)
    l.   bright lilac (June 9, 1967)
    m.   pale lilac (cyl. 2, 1967)

36. 4d. ultramarine (February 7, 1966)
    a. white flaw over top leaf at left (R3/6)
    b. retouched

        Watermark as above. Phosphor lines.
37. 3d. pale mauve (June 9, 1967)
    a. deep mauve (1967)
    b. brownish mauve (1967)
    c. vertical strip with design missing from bottom stamp
38. 4d. ultramarine (September 5, 1967)
    a. retouched leaf flaw

     No watermark. Chalky paper. Phosphor lines. PVA gum.
39. 4d. sepia (September 4, 1968)
    a. retouched leaf flaw
40. 4d. red (February 26, 1969)
41. 5d. Stuart blue (September 4, 1968)
    a. white dot above lowest leaf at right (R16/6)
    b. leaf joined to coat-of-arms (R12/12)

	CYLINDER NUMBERS (all no dot)		
2½d.	No. 1	4d. blue	No. 1
3d.	No. 1	4d. blue	No. 1 (Phosphor)
3d.	No. 2	4d. sepia	No. 1
3d.	No. 2 (Phosphor)	4d. red	No. 1
		5d.	No. 1

ADVISORY COMMITTEES

Members of the advisory committees and the positions they held at the time were:

Guernsey
A. M. Mackay (Chairman), Member of the Guernsey Art Committee.
Lt.-Col. W. Byam, Philatelist and Art Connoisseur.
J. M. Y. Trotter, Postal Historian and Heraldic Expert.

The Rev. F. W. Cogman ⎫
T. Oscar Guilbert   ⎬ Members of the Guernsey Art
The Rev. G. A. James   ⎭ Committee
J. R. D. Jones

Jersey

Major E. P. Le Masurier (Chairman), President of the Société Jersiaise, a former jurat and Lt. Bailiff of Jersey.

G. A. Candlin, States Deputy and President of the States Finance Committee.

E. Huelin, former States Deputy.

R. Hyland, Representative of the Chamber of Commerce on the Advisory Committee for Post Office Services in Jersey.

W. H. Krichefski, States Senator, member of the Advisory Committee for Post Office Services in Jersey.

C. P. Rumfitt, States Senator, President of the States Tourism Committee.

12

THE INDEPENDENT POSTAL SERVICES

When the British Post Office announced in 1967 that it was to become a public corporation in 1969 it gave the States of Guernsey and Jersey the opportunity of running their own postal services if they wished to do so. Both Islands set up committees to investigate the possibilities. They commissioned a firm of accountants from London to cost the schemes for them and eventually decided to opt for postal independence. After the Postmaster General had satisfied himself that proper arrangements had been made for the future of the staff, their pensions, etc., he agreed to the transfer of the services to the Islands.

Both Islands appointed the Crown Agents to handle their stamp issues, artists were commissioned, and contracts were placed with printers.

Guernsey's Issues

FIRST DEFINITIVES, 1969

Guernsey appointed Richard Granger Barrett to design her stamps. After visiting Guernsey and discussing designs with the Postal Committee, Mr. Granger Barrett went to the British Museum to inspect coins bearing the heads of British monarchs who were to be featured on the stamps. Plaster casts were made of the coins and from these the heads were prepared. For the central vignettes local views, the island crests of the Bailiwick, a map, and the Guernsey lily were chosen, and the Machin portrait of the Queen was selected for the right-hand panels.

The contract for printing the stamps was placed with Imprimerie

12.1   First definitives

Delrieu of Paris, but because of technical difficulties they printed only the three high values and the contract for the values to 2s. 6d. was transferred to Harrison & Sons Ltd.

The stamps (Figure 12.1) were issued on October 1, 1969, the day that the States of Guernsey took over from the British Post Office. Technical details are given below.

Low values, ½d. to 2s. 6d. printed in photogravure by Harrison & Sons Ltd., no watermark, perforated 14, all multicoloured:

½d., Castle Cornet and Edward the Confessor; 1d., William I and map of the Bailiwick; 1½d., Martello Tower and Henry II; 2d., Sark Crest and John; 3d., Alderney Crest and Edward III; 4d., Guernsey Lily and Henry V; 5d., Guernsey Crest and Elizabeth 1; 6d., Alderney Crest and Charles II; 9d., Sark Crest and George III; 1s., Guernsey Crest and Victoria; 1s. 6d. Map and William I; 1s. 9d., Guernsey Lily and Elizabeth I; 2s. 6d. Martello Tower and John. Cylinder numbers (figures and A or B) appeared twice on each sheet.

High values, 5s. to £1, printed in photogravure by Imprimerie Delrieu, Paris, no watermark, perforated 12, all multicoloured:

5s., Sark Harbour; 10s., Alderney Harbour, £1, St. Peter Port Harbour. The date 20.6.1969 appeared in the bottom left corner of the sheets.

Values to 2s. 6d. are in sheets of 60 (two panes of 6 × 5 divided by a gutter margin) and the higher values in sheets of 30 (6 × 5).

Official first-day covers and presentation packs were issued on October 1, 1969. Exceptionally, some stamps were cancelled to order contrary to regulations.

Numbers Printed

Numbers printed of the definitives were: ½d., 2,480,000; 1d., 900,000; 1d. (redrawn), 1,160,000; 1½d., 980,000; 2d., 420,000; 3d., 426,000; 4d., 6,987,000; 5d., 3,390,000; 6d., 450,000; 9d., 450,000; 1s., 450,000; 1s. 6d., 450,000; 1s. 6d. (redrawn), 610,000; 1s. 9d., 300,000; 2s. 6d., 240,000; 5s., 210,000; 10s., 114,000; £1, 120,000.

Errors

The only major error reported on the sheet stamps is the 1s. 9d. with the dark green colour missing from the stem of the Guernsey Lily. A pane of 30 was found by a London dealer.

The 1d. and 1s. 6d. were issued with the wrong latitude on the map of Guernsey. It was given as 40°, 30′ W instead of 49°, 30′ W. This was corrected on a new printing issued on February 4, 1970. The 1d. with incorrect latitude is found from cylinders 1A 1A and 2A 2A. The 1d. and 1s. 6d. are also known with an extra line of latitude (row 1, stamp 2, cylinder 1A) and with the line partly removed.

Varieties

The 1d. and 1s. 6d. with corrected latitude are reported with an extra circle to the top left of the compass (row 4, stamp 3). Two other varieties occur on the 1d. only: a 'dagger' flaw in the King's shoulder (row 4, stamp 1) and broken U in LIHOU (row 5, stamp 3).

Booklets

Three stamp booklets with panes of 4d., 5d., and 1d. stamps printed as singles with selvedge all round were issued on December 12, 1969. They feature Guernsey Militia on the covers: 2s., Trooper Royal Guernsey Cavalry (Light Dragoons) 1814; 4s., Officer St. Martin's Company (La Milice Bleue) 1720; 6s., Colour Sergeant of Grenadiers and Rifleman East (Town) Regiment, Guernsey 1833. The booklets were printed by Harrison & Sons Ltd. in sheets of 48 (6 × 8) and cut into singles. The contents are: 2s., 3 @ 4d., 2 @ 5d., 2 @ 1d.; 4s., 6 @ 4d., 4 @ 5d., 4 @ 1d.; 6s., 9 @ 4d., 6 @ 5d., 6 @ 1d. The 1d. stamps showed the correct latitude.

Two major errors were found in these booklets. In about twenty of the 4s. booklets a pane of the 4d. stamp was found with the dark green missing from the stem of the Guernsey Lily. In three of the 2s. booklets a pane of the 4d. was found with the yellow missing from the stamens of the Guernsey Lily. Colour shifts of both varieties also exist.

New booklets with the same contents but showing different Militiamen were issued on June 29, 1970. The designs were printed in different colours and they show the following subjects: 2s., Officer, Royal Guernsey Horse Artillery, 1793; 4s., Gunner, Royal Guernsey Artillery, 1743; 6s., Sergeant Rifles, 1st Guernsey Light Infantry, 1832.

One major error has been found in the 4s. booklet, where the 5d.

has the gold missing. Another booklet had the crest on the 5d. shifted to the right panel over the Queen's portrait.

New Perforations

New printings of the 10s. and £1 definitives were issued on March 4, 1970, with the perforations changed to $13\frac{1}{4} \times 13$, to make for easier separation. Numbers printed were 55,200 of each.

Papers

The first printings of the values to 2s. 6d. were on a thick esparto paper. Later printings were on a thinner, whiter wood-free paper (wood-free is a technical term meaning a paper made entirely from wood pulp). These papers are listed in the standard catalogues as thick and thin respectively.

COMMEMORATIVES

The first commemorative stamps issued by Guernsey were a series of four which appeared on December 1, 1969, for the bicentenary of the birth of *General Sir Isaac Brock* (Figure 12.2). They were designed by Richard Granger Barrett and offset–lithographed by Format International Security Printers on unwatermarked paper perforated $13\frac{1}{2} \times 14$. The designs featured: 4d., Colonel Isaac Brock; 5d., Major General Sir Isaac Brock; 1s. 9d. Ensign Isaac Brock; 2s. 6d., Post-humous Arms and Supporters and Flags. All were multicoloured.

12.2   General Sir Isaac Brock

167

An official first-day cover and presentation pack was issued. The set was withdrawn from sale on February 28, 1970.

On May 9, 1970 three stamps were issued for the twenty-fifth anniversary of the *Liberation* (Figure 12.3). Designed by staff artists of Courvoisier, Switzerland, from photographs, they were printed in photogravure by Courvoisier on unwatermarked paper with silk threads and perforated $11\frac{3}{4} \times 11\frac{1}{2}$. The designs feature: 4d. blue, Royal Naval Landing Craft 103 entering St. Peter Port Harbour, with aircraft overhead; 5d. red, the arrival of the Royal Navy in the roadsteads; 1s. 6d. brown, Brigadier A. E. Snow reading the Royal Proclamation from the steps of Elizabeth College. An official first-day cover and presentation pack was issued.

A series publicizing *agriculture and horticulture* was issued on August 12, 1970. Designed by Courvoisier artists from subjects submitted by the Guernsey Post Office Board, they were printed on unwatermarked paper with silk threads and perforated $11\frac{1}{2}$. The designs (Figure 12.4) feature: 4d., The Guernsey Tom(tomatoes); 5d., Guernsey Cow; 9d., Guernsey Bull; 1s. 6d., Freesias. All were multicoloured. An official first-day cover and presentation pack was issued. A cover was also issued by the Tomato Marketing Board.

For *Christmas*, 1970, a series was issued on November 11. Designed by Courvoisier from subjects submitted by the Post Office Board, they were printed in photogravure on unwatermarked paper with silk threads, perforated $11\frac{1}{2}$. The designs (Figure 12.5) feature: 4d., St. Anne's Church, Alderney; 5d., St. Peter Port Church; 9d., St.

12.3   Anniversary of Liberation

12.4 Agriculture and horticulture

Peter's Church, Sark; 1s. 6d. St. Tugual's Chapel, Herm. All were multicoloured. An official first-day cover and presentation pack was issued.

On June 2, 1971, Guernsey commemorated one of its illustrious citizens, *Thomas De La Rue* (1793–1866), whose name is so familiar to philatelists. The series of four each reproduced a stamp printed by the firm of De La Rue: 2p., olive-grey (Hong Kong 2c. of 1862); $2\frac{1}{2}$p., carmine-red (Great Britain 4d. of 1855–57); 4p., deep bluish-green (Italy 5c. of 1862); $7\frac{1}{2}$p., deep blue (Confederate States 5c. of 1862). The stamps were recess-printed by De La Rue and perf. $14 \times 13\frac{1}{2}$. The 2p. is reported in a major shade variety of red-brown.

The Guernsey *Christmas* 1971 series was announced for issue on October 27. It features churches once again (2p., $2\frac{1}{2}$p., 5p., $7\frac{1}{2}$p.). The 1972 programme has been given as February 10, Mail Packet Ships (first series); May 22, Guernsey Cattle Breeders Conference overprint, 5p. on 1970 9d. agriculture; May 24, Wild Flowers (first series); and October 25, Stained Glass.

DECIMAL DEFINITIVES, 1971

Guernsey adopted decimal currency on the same day as Britain (February 15, 1971). In consequence the 1969 definitives were re-

12.5 Christmas 1970

issued in new denominations in two batches. On January 6, 1971, came the three higher values: 10p. (formerly the 2s. 6d.); 20p. (as 5s.); and 50p. (as 10s.). These, together with the unchanged top value of £1, were printed photogravure by Imprimerie Delrieu, Paris, in sheets of 30. The perforations were: 14 for the 10p. and $13\frac{1}{4} \times 13$ for the others.

The remaining values appeared on February 15, 1971. The denominations (former values in brackets) were:

$\frac{1}{2}$p. ($\frac{1}{2}$d.); 1p. (1d.); 1$\frac{1}{2}$p. (1$\frac{1}{2}$d.); 2p. (4d.); 2$\frac{1}{2}$p. (5d.); 3p. (3d.); 3$\frac{1}{2}$p. (1s. 9d.); 4p. (2d.); 5p. (1s. 6d.); 6p. (6d.); 7$\frac{1}{2}$p. (1s.); 9p. (9d.).

The stamps were printed photogravure by Harrison & Sons Ltd. in sheets of 50 (two panes of 25), perforated 14. The 1$\frac{1}{2}$p., 2p., 2$\frac{1}{2}$p., and 3p. have multipurpose coating.

Three presentation packs were issued: $\frac{1}{2}$p. to 4p.; 5p. to 9p.; and 10p. to 50p. Three first-day covers were also provided.

Decimal booklets

New stamp booklets with different covers, featuring further Guernsey Militia uniforms, were issued on February 15, 1971, as follows: 10p., Officer, Royal Guernsey Horse Artillery, 1850; 20p., Sergeant, Guernsey Light Infantry, 1826; 30p., Sergeant and Bandsman, Royal Guernsey Light Infantry (North Regiment), 1866. The contents were: 10p., 2 @ $\frac{1}{2}$p., 2 @ 2p., 2 @ 2$\frac{1}{2}$p.; 20p., 4 @ $\frac{1}{2}$p., 4 @ 2p., 4 @ 2$\frac{1}{2}$p.; 30p., 6 @ $\frac{1}{2}$p., 6 @ 2p., 6 @ 2$\frac{1}{2}$p.

Guernsey abolished two-tier postal rates on Decimalization Day. Mail paid at 2$\frac{1}{2}$p. (up to 4 oz) is now carried First Class to Jersey and to the U.K. Local mail within the Bailiwick of Guernsey costs 2p.

POSTAGE DUES

12.6 Postage due

A series of seven postage dues was issued on October 1, 1969; they were designed by R. Granger Barrett and photogravure-printed by Imprimerie Delrieu in sheets of 120 (two panes of 60: 10 × 6), perforated 12$\frac{1}{2}$ × 12. The design features Castle Cornet and the denominations are overprinted in large black open figures: 1d. plum; 2d. green; 3d. red; 4d. blue; 5d. ochre; 6d. blue-green; and 1s. brown (Figure 12.6). Numbers printed were: 1d., 420,000; others, 210,000 of each.

A decimal series in the same design and colours was issued on February 15, 1971, in denominations of ½p., 1p., 2p., 3p., 4p., 5p., 10p. A presentation pack was issued in 1971 to hold both sets.

POSTAL STATIONERY

The postal stationery comprises three registered envelopes in the G, H, and K sizes without stamps and a 9d. aerogramme printed by McCorquodale with impressed 9d. stamp, showing St. Peter Port Harbour as depicted on the £1 stamp. For decimalization the aerogramme was surcharged 4p. and issued on February 15, 1971. Some are reported with albino overprint. A 5p. form with the stamp showing Sark Harbour was issued on July 1, 1971. On September 11, 1971, 50,000 air letters were overprinted for the Guernsey Scout Jubilee.

Official Stationery

Four sizes of envelope are used by the Guernsey Post Office with the Guernsey Arms and POSTAGE PAID in a rectangular frame. They are numbered 1, 2, 3, and 4. There are also adhesive labels with the official frank, numbered L1 and L2, and one in blue with registration lines numbered L2.

The Philatelic Bureau uses an envelope with the Guernsey map frank (*see* below) in blue and a registered envelope with the same frank.

CANCELLATIONS

A completely new series of postal markings and cancellations was introduced by the new postal administration.

The Head Office has several single circles of 27mm diameter, all with 'Guernsey Post Office' round the top, and blank at the bottom (Figure 12.7). There is also a similar type with 'Philatelic Bureau' at the bottom. For counter work, handstamps are used lettered from E to N (except I).

A single-circle type of 22mm diameter with GUERNSEY POST OFFICE round the circumference and a bar at the bottom, with the time and date in three lines (sometimes there is a line instead of the time), is

12.7

12.8

12.9

12.10

12.11

used in the cancelling machine. This was used first of all with the old slogan GUERNSEY/THE BRITISH HOLIDAY ABROAD and later with wavy lines (Figure 12.8). The slogan was withdrawn on December 12, 1969.

There is a single-circle rubber stamp of 30mm diameter with 'Guernsey Post Office' at the top, a star between two lines at the bottom, and the date and time in two lines (Figure 12.9).

A rectangular parcel stamp measuring 53 × 37mm and reading GUERNSEY POST OFFICE/PARCEL POST/(DATE) HEAD OFFICE was introduced on July 20, 1970. The old British parcel stamp was used prior to this date.

For registration the old British oval type was used alongside a new oval type inscribed 'Guernsey Post Office/Registered' (Figure 12.10) for several months until it was replaced by a new oval type inscribed REGISTERED/GUERNSEY POST OFFICE.

For bulk postings there is a red handstamp of 30mm diameter with 'Guernsey Post Office' at the top and the word PAID above the date (Figure 12.11). Two machine cancellations have the small circular datestamp struck in red, with wavy lines which have either 1ST PAID or 2ND PAID in the centre (Figure 12.12). The '1ST' and '2ND' were removed when two-tier postage was abolished on February 15, 1971.

Firms and government department meters carry, beside the datestamp, a boxed stamp with a map of the Bailiwick and rising sun with the inscription 'Guernsey Postage Paid', a number, and the denomination (Figure 12.13). For large rebate postings of Francis Hodgson Ltd. a printed boxed frank of this type is used in red or black with 'Serial 1' instead of a denomination (Figure 12.14). In the summer of 1970 this was replaced (Figure 12.15) by a red boxed GUERNSEY/POSTAGE/2nd/PAID.

Some official letters from the Guernsey Postal Administration are marked with either a boxed ON POSTAL SERVICE or, for international mail, with a boxed SERVICE DES POSTES.

The first slogan cancellation used by the new administration was a boxed one reading OBESITY/SHORTENS LIFE/TREAT IT SERIOUSLY, which was used on a number of occasions from May 26, 1970, onwards on large mailings organized by Medical Mailing International on behalf of Servier Laboratories Ltd. This was replaced on February 1, 1971,

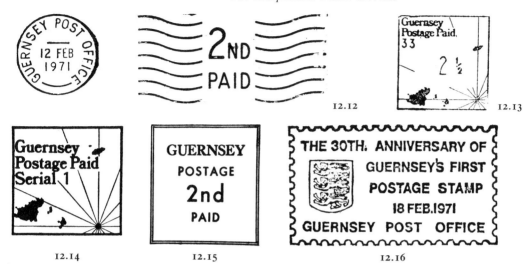

12.12

12.13

12.14 12.15 12.16

by one reading STAMP OUT OVERWEIGHT, which was also used on
later dates.

The commemorative cancellations issued to date are as follows.
A single circle of 23mm diameter, with 'Guernsey Post Office' at the
top, 'First Day of Issue' at the bottom, and the date in a single line in
the centre with 'Philatelic Bureau' in two lines below it, was used on
October 1, 1969; December 1, 1969; May 9, 1970; August 12, 1970;
November 11, 1970; January 6, 1971; and February 15, 1971. A
single circle of 25mm diameter with 'Guernsey Post Office' round
the top, 'Oldest Pillar Box in British Isles' round the bottom, and
'1853–1970/9 FEB 1970/Union Street' in three lines in the centre,
commemorated the 117th anniversary of the pillar box. On February 18, 1971, a boxed handstamp (Figure 12.16) commemorated
the thirtieth anniversary of Guernsey's first 1d. stamp of 1941. One
issued on April 7, 1971, commemorated the thirtieth anniversary of
the first ½d. stamp of 1941. From May 12 to 18, 1971 a slogan
was used for the Annual Conference of the Royal Liver Society. On
June 2 a small boxed handstamp showing an old printing press was
used for the first day of issue of the De La Rue stamps. On June 3 a
circular handstamp containing a reproduction of the famous scroll
marking of 1810–30 was used for the opening of the new Postal
Museum and Philatelic Bureau in Smith Street. This continues in use.

On September 4/5, 1971 a special cancellation was used for the Guernsey Power Boat Race and on September 11 one for the Diamond Jubilee of the Guernsey Scouts Association.

The envelope slogan 'First Day of Issue', used by the British Post Office, continues in use with the 'Guernsey Post Office' datestamp. It was used in the ordinary position, with the datestamp at the left, on December 1, 1969, on the Brock issue, and transposed on August 12, 1970, on the Agriculture and succeeding issues.

Because mail sent at the $2\frac{1}{2}$p. rate to England was being treated as second class by some British delivery offices, a slogan reading FIRST CLASS/MAIL, with the Arms of Guernsey on either side of the MAIL, was put into use on May 21, 1971, and continued until July 2. It will be used again if it is considered necessary.

Sub-Offices

New datestamps were issued to the twenty sub-offices on October 1, 1969. They were of $22\frac{1}{2}$mm diameter with 'Guernsey Post Office' at the top and the name of the office at the bottom (Figure 12.17).

12.17

The offices are: Alderney, Braye Road, Catel, Cobo, Forest, Herm Island, Les Gravées, L'Islet, Market Place, St. Andrew, St. John's, St. Martin, St. Peter-in-the-Wood, St. Sampson, St. Saviour, Sark, Torteval, Vale, Vale Road, Ville au Roi.

The Alderney stamp was replaced by one of $26\frac{1}{2}$mm diameter in December, 1969, the Sark stamp on November 11, 1970, and the Herm on January 6, 1971. Some other offices also have $26\frac{1}{2}$mm stamps for counter work. Those seen are Market Place and St. Sampson but there may be others.

Single-circle rubber stamps of 30mm diameter were issued for use on small packets on June 16, 1970, to the islands of Alderney, Herm, and Sark.

Parcel stamps measuring 53×36mm were issued on July 20, 1970, to all twenty sub-offices. *See* Figure 12.18.

Commemorative cancellations of 23mm diameter were used in Alderney, Herm, and Sark for the first day of the Christmas stamps on November 11, 1970.

Charge Markings

British and Regional stamps were invalidated after October 31,

---

GUERNSEY POST OFFICE
PARCEL POST

1 5 MAY 1970

VILLE AU ROI

12.18 Advance proof of parcel post cancellation

1969, but this was extended by the Guernsey Post Office until about March, 1970. From then onwards double postage was charged on letters bearing them and an unframed handstamp STAMP INVALID was applied in black. Later a large boxed stamp divided in two vertical panels with D and space for a manuscript figure at the left and TO PAY/POSTED/UNPAID at the right was struck in green. A plastic label reading GUERNSEY POSTAGE STAMPS ONLY MAY BE USED ON ITEMS POSTED IN THIS BOX was stuck on all pillar boxes.

A small green handstamp with TO PAY POSTED UNPAID was used from May, 1970, on letters from Rhodesia with stamps not recognized by the British Government.

At the time of writing, a framed handstamp STAMP INVALID is applied in violet to letters with British or Regional stamps.

Jersey's Issues

FIRST DEFINITIVES, 1969

Jersey's stamps were designed by Victor Whiteley. The States of Jersey Department of Postal Administration decided that it wanted local views on its definitives and supplied pictures of these for the vignettes. Whitely designed a special standard border to run down the right-hand side and across the bottom of thirteen of the fifteen denominations. This incorporated a portrait of the Queen, specially taken by Cecil Beaton, and featured seagulls, a lighthouse, boats, a lobster and lobster pot, and other marine life. The Arms of Jersey appeared in the bottom left corner. The other two denominations were of vertical format and featured the Beaton portrait of the Queen with decorative borders.

Contracts for printing the stamps were placed with Harrison & Sons Ltd. for values to 1s. 9d. and with Courvoisier, of Switzerland, for the four high values.

The stamps (Figure 12.19) were issued on October 1, 1969, the day the States of Jersey took over from the British Post Office. Technical details are given below.

Low values, $\frac{1}{2}$d. to 1s. 9d. printed in photogravure by Harrison & Sons Ltd., no watermark, perforated 14, all multicoloured:

12.19 First definitives

½d., Elizabeth Castle; 1d., La Hougue Bie; 2d., Portelet Bay; 3d., La Corbière Lighthouse; 4d., Mont Orgueil Castle by night; 5d., Arms and Royal Mace; 6d., Jersey Cow; 9d., map of Jersey; 1s., Mont Orgueil Castle by day; 1s. 6d., map of Jersey; 1s. 9d., portrait of the Queen. Cylinder numbers appeared in all four corners of the sheets.

High values, 2s. 6d. to £1, printed in photogravure by Courvoisier, Switzerland, no watermark, perforated 12, all multi-coloured:

2s. 6d., the Airport; 5s., States Chamber; 10s., Royal Court; £1, portrait of the Queen.

Values to 1s. 9d. were printed in sheets of 60(6 × 10) and the high values in sheets of 25(5 × 5).

There is only one major error in the sheet-printed stamps, the 1d. with yellow missing from the leopards, but there are a few colour shifts and misplaced perforations. There are also a few minor constant flaws.

Official first-day covers and presentation packs were issued on October 1, 1969.

Imperforate Proofs

A few imperforate proofs exist in the issued colours. These were presented to members of the States Postal Committee. They were not valid for postage.

Booklets

Three stamp booklets were issued on October 1, 1969. The 2s. had single panes of the 4d. and 1d. printed with selvedge all round. It had a blue cover with a map on the front and was printed in sheets of 48 (6 × 8) by Harrisons and cut into singles. One booklet in each 48 had cylinder numbers on the 4d. panes.

The 7s. booklets with yellow covers, showing the Arms and Mace, and 10s. booklets with pink covers, showing Mont Orgueil Castle, were also printed by Harrisons with strips of ten stamps from the left and right sheet margins. They were cut into single booklets containing vertical pairs of stamps and half the booklets had the stamps inverted. The contents of the booklets are: 2s., 5 @ 4d., 4 @ 1d.; 7s., 12 @ 4d., 6 @ 5d., 6 @ 1d.; 10s., 14 @ 4d., 12 @ 5d., 4 @ 1d.

Papers

The first printings of the values to 1s. 9d. were on a thick esparto paper. Later printings were on a thinner, whiter wood-free paper. These papers are listed in the standard catalogues as thick and thin respectively.

COMMEMORATIVES

Jersey's first commemoratives were the series of four stamps issued on October 1, 1969, for the inauguration of the *Independent Postal Service* (Figure 12.20). They were designed by R. G. Sellar and printed in photogravure by Harrison & Sons Ltd. on unwatermarked paper, perforated 14. The design features a first-day cover with the inscription 'To Friends of all Nations—Greetings!' The denominations are 4d., 5d., 1s. 6d., and 1s. 9d. The Philatelic Bureau dispatched 33,500 first-day covers and a presentation pack was issued. Unsold remainders were destroyed on January 20, 1971.

On May 9, 1970, four multicoloured stamps were issued for the twenty-fifth anniversary of the *Liberation* (Figure 12.21). Designed by Rosalind Dease from paintings, they were printed in photogravure by Courvoisier on unwatermarked paper with silk threads and perforated 11½: 4d., Lord Coutanche, the wartime Bailiff, by Sir James Gunn; 5d., Sir Winston Churchill by D. Van Praag; 1s. 6d., '*Liberation*', by Edmund Blampied; 1s. 9d., the s.s. Vega, by an unknown artist. The Bureau dispatched over 53,000 official first-day covers and issued over 11,000 presentation packs. A special presentation pack in red and gold was distributed to 10,000 school-children in addition. The stamps were withdrawn on May 9, 1971.

For the *Battle of Flowers* a series of four was issued on July 28, 1970 (Figure 12.22). Designed by Jennifer Toombs from winners of the 1969 Battle they were printed in photogravure by Courvoisier on unwatermarked paper with silk threads and perforated 11½: 4d., Noddy in Toyland; 5d., Rags to Riches; 1s. 6d., Gourmet's Delight; 1s. 9d., We're the Greatest. All were multicoloured. An official first-day cover and presentation pack was issued.

A series featuring *wild life* from the Jersey Zoo was issued on March 12, 1971 (Figure 12.23). It was designed by Jennifer Toombs and printed in photogravure by Courvoisier on unwatermarked

12.20 Independent postal service

12.21 Anniversary of Liberation

12.22 Battle of Flowers

12.23 Wildlife

paper with silk threads and perforated $11\frac{1}{2}$: 2p., White-eared Pheasant; $2\frac{1}{2}$p. Thick-billed Parrot; $7\frac{1}{2}$p., Ursine Colobus Monkey; 9p., Ring-tailed Lemur. All were multicoloured.

The Golden Jubilee of the Royal British Legion was commemorated with a set of four on June 15, 1971. Designed by Gordon Drummond and lithographed by a new printer (Questa Colour Security Printers Ltd.) the values were: 2p., Legion Badge; $2\frac{1}{2}$p., Poppy emblem and Flanders field; $7\frac{1}{2}$p., Jack Counter, v.c., and Victoria Cross; 9p., Union Jack and Tricolour and British and French steel helmets. All were multicoloured and perf. 14.

A series featuring paintings by Jersey artists was issued on October 5, 1971. Printed in multicoloured photogravure by Courvoisier, the denominations are 2p., Tante Elizabeth, by Edmund Blampied (1886–1966); $2\frac{1}{2}$p., The English Fleet in the Channel, by Peter Monamy (1670–1749); $7\frac{1}{2}$p., The Boyhood of Raleigh, by Sir John Millais, p.r.a. (1829–1896); 9p., The Blind Beggar, by W. W. Oulness, r.a. (1848–1933).

Future issues (announced while this book was in the press) include a series for the Royal Jersey Militia, an issue featuring wild flowers, a second series for the Jersey Wildlife Preservation Trust, and an issue for the Queen's Silver Wedding.

Imperforate Proofs

Imperforate proofs of all commemoratives in the issued colours were printed in small quantities for presentation to members of the Jersey Postal Committee. They were not valid for postage.

DECIMAL DEFINITIVES

With decimalization the 1969 definitives were re-issued in the new currency. On October 1, 1970, appeared the 10p. (as 2s. 6d.), 20p. (as 5s.), and 50p. (as 10s.). Together with the unchanged £1 they were printed by Courvoisier in sheets of 25 (5 × 5), perforated 12.

The low values were issued on February 15, 1971, taking the original designs shown in brackets:

$\frac{1}{2}$p. ($\frac{1}{2}$d.); 1p. (3d.); $1\frac{1}{2}$p. (6d.); 2p. (4d.); $2\frac{1}{2}$p. (5d.); 3p. (1d.); $3\frac{1}{2}$p. (2d.); 4p (9d.); 5p. (1s.); 6p. (new design: Martello Tower at Archirondel); $7\frac{1}{2}$p. (1s. 6d.); 9p. (1s. 9d.)

They were printed by Harrison & Sons Ltd. in sheets of 50 (5 × 10), perforated 14.

Official first-day covers and presentation packs were issued.

Decimal booklets

Decimal booklets were also issued on February 15, 1971:

10p. (2 @ 2½p., 2 @ 2p., 2 @ ½p.)—blue cover with Martello Tower at Archirondel. Single panes with selvedge on two sides only.

35p. (6 @ 2½p., 10 @ 2p.)—yellow cover with Royal Court. Stamps in vertical pairs from left and right sheet margins.

50p. (12 @ 2½p., 10 @ 2p.)—pink cover with Elizabeth Castle. Stamps in vertical pairs from left and right sheet margins.

The 2½p. stamp in the 10p. booklet has been reported with gold mace missing from the design; also with doubling of the mace.

Jersey abolished the two-tier system of rates on decimalization. Mail paid at 2½p. (up to 4 oz) is treated as First Class to the other Channel Islands and to the U.K. Inter-island mails costs 2p.

POSTAGE DUES

A series of six postage dues was issued on October 1, 1969; they were designed by F. W. Guenier and offset-lithographed by Bradbury, Wilkinson & Co. Ltd. in sheets of 120 (two panes of 60: 6 × 10), perforated 14 × 13½. The 1d., 2d., and 3d. feature numerals in a double-ringed circle and the 1s., 2s. 6d., and 5s. a map of Jersey (Figures 12.24 and 12.25).

Shades exist of the 1d., 1s., and 2s. 6d. and the 1d. is known with double horizontal perforations.

A decimal series in the map design was issued on February 15, 1971, in denominations of ½p., 1p., 2p., 3p., 4p., 5p., 10p., and 14p. They are in sheets of 50, perforated 14 × 13½.

POSTAL STATIONERY

The postal stationery comprises three registered envelopes in the G, H, and K sizes with an embossed 3s. 5d. stamp in blue in a Tudor rose design and a 9d. aerogramme printed by McCorquodale with impressed 9d. stamp featuring the map design of the 9d. adhesive.

12.24

12.25

Postage dues

For decimalization the registered envelopes were printed with an embossed 17p. stamp and the aerogramme with an impressed 4p. stamp. A 5p. airletter was issued on July 1, 1971. It features Mont Orgueil.

CANCELLATIONS

There have been few changes in cancellations under the new postal administration. For the most part it has been content to continue

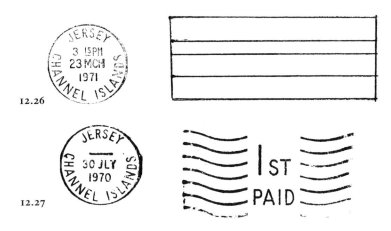

12.26

12.27

using the old British handstamps.

At the Head Office a new machine cancellation in the form of a box measuring 51 × 22mm and containing three unevenly spaced horizontal lines was put into use on December 1, 1969 (Figure 12.26). The datestamp continued unchanged and the holiday slogans used by the British Post Office continue in use.

A new single-circle rubber stamp of 30mm diameter with JERSEY at the top, CHANNEL ISLANDS at the bottom, and the date between two horizontal bars across the centre was introduced in December, 1969, for use on small packets.

In March, 1970, 25-mm and 27-mm single-circle plastic cancellations inscribed PHILATELIC SERVICE at the top, CHANNEL ISLANDS at the bottom, and the date and JERSEY in two lines across the centre were introduced for use on stamps sold cancelled to order. There are similar stamps inscribed PHILATELIC BUREAU for use on Bureau mail. These are *not* used for cancelling to order.

A new parcel cancellation was put into use in July, 1970. It is a single-circle rubber stamp, 30mm in diameter, with PARCEL POST round the top, CHANNEL ISLANDS round the bottom, and JERSEY and the date in two lines in the centre.

For bulk postings the machine cancellations have the datestamp struck in red, with wavy lines which have either 1ST PAID or 2ND PAID in the centre (Figure 12.27). When the two-tier service was

12.28

12.29

discontinued in February, 1971, one reading POSTAGE PAID was put into use.

Firms and government department meters carry, beside the date-stamp, a heavy three-sided frame with the Arms of Jersey in a box at the top and two uncoloured wavy lines at the sides, with JERSEY and a serial number at the bottom and the denomination, in numerals only, in the centre (Figure 12.28). There is also an oblong type with the Arms in the top left corner (Figure 12.29).

The only slogan cancellation introduced by the new administration was JERSEY WELCOMES/THE/ARCHBISHOP OF CANTERBURY/31ST JULY – 4TH AUGUST, used in the transposed position during the five days of the Archbishop's visit in 1970.

Quite a number of commemorative cancellations have been used. The first was the shield type used for the first day of issue of the new definitives on October 1, 1969. Then came a large single circle, 36mm

in diameter, inscribed ENGLAND – AUSTRALIA at the top, 50TH ANNI-
VERSARY FLIGHT at the bottom, and JERSEY/2 DEC 69/CHANNEL
ISLANDS in the centre, for the fiftieth anniversary of the Ross Smith
Flight in 1919.

A special cancellation in the form of an outline map of Jersey was
used on mail posted on board the Swedish cruise liner M.S. *Kungsholm* when it called at Jersey on May 5, and September 28, 1970,
and on board the sister ship M.S. *Gripsholm* when it called on August
14, 1970. The map design was also used for the Trustee Savings Bank
Conference held in Jersey on May 20, 1970, when a posting box was
provided at the Hotel de France.

A large rectangular cancellation with the emblem of the Dunkirk
Veterans Association and the inscription SALUTE TO THE MEN OF
DUNKIRK. 19th JUNE 1970 JERSEY CHANNEL ISLANDS was used on June
19, 1970, for the thirtieth anniversary of the withdrawal of the
British Expeditionary Force from Dunkirk in 1940.

The 25-mm Philatelic Bureau cancellation was used on a small
quantity of commemorative covers posted on August 18, 1970, to
mark the opening of the Jersey Office of Interlink Development
Ltd., Jersey's publicity agents.

A privately sponsored handstamp in the shape of a 50p. coin, with
Mont Orgueil Castle and the date in the centre and FIRST ISSUE OF
JERSEY DECIMAL STAMPS round the frame, was used on October 1,
1970, on the decimal high values.

A large rectangular cancellation with the first Jersey railway engine
and the inscription JERSEY CHANNEL ISLANDS/26 OCT 70/JERSEY/RAIL-
WAY/COMPANY/1870–1970 was used on October 26, 1970, on mail
from the Railway Centenary Exhibition, Société Jersiaise Museum.

A single-circle cancellation of 25mm, with FIRST DAY OF ISSUE
round the top, JERSEY CHANNEL ISLANDS round the bottom, and the
date and PHILATELIC SERVICE in three lines in the centre has been used
on the following commemorative issues: May 9, 1970 (Liberation),
July 28, 1970 (Battle of Flowers), October 1, 1970 (decimal high
values), February 15, 1971 (decimal low values), and March 12, 1971
(Jersey Wild Life). The old British envelope 'First Day of Issue'
slogan was used on covers bearing single stamps of the first definitives,
the Inauguration of the Jersey Post Office, the Liberation, and Battle
of Flowers issues.

12.30

For the opening of Jersey's new Postal Headquarters at Mont Millais a slogan cancellation reading Opening of Jersey's/New Postal H.Q./February, 1971 was used on February 4, 1971. A special postmark was used at the New York philatelic exhibition 'INTERPEX' on March 12, 1971 (Figure 12.30).

On April 1, 1971, a special handstamp was used to commemorate the thirtieth anniversary of Jersey's first 1d. stamp introduced in 1941.

A circular pictorial cancellation was used on May 6, August 15, and October 1, 1971, on mail posted on board the liner *Kungsholm* and on August 7 on mail posted on board the *Gripsholm*.

On May 6, 1971, a rectangular cancellation was used for the Imperial Life of Canada Convention.

On May 15, 1971, the 'Lions' postmark was used; it is a large rectangular type with a cannon, inscribed SIEGE OF GOREY CASTLE 1643 & 1654/15 MAY/1971/GOREY . JERSEY/CHANNEL ISLANDS. It was for a re-enactment of the sieges, set up by the Lions Organization of Jersey.

A special handstamp marked the visit of Cardinal Heenan. It read: Visit of Cardinal Heenan Archbishop of Westminster, 12th June, 1971, Jersey, Channel Islands.

On October 2 a rectangular postmark incorporating the Jersey Scroll of 1810–30 was used for the Postal History Society's Annual Conference. Special commemorative covers and postcards were produced for the occasion.

Charge Markings

British and Regional stamps were invalidated after October 31, 1969, and letters bearing them were marked with an unframed handstamp STAMP VOID in green and charged double postage. This was replaced in 1970 with a framed handstamp STAMP INVALID, which was struck in violet. This, in turn was replaced with a boxed violet stamp reading STAMP INVALID/8d. TO PAY.

A plastic label inscribed in red ONLY JERSEY STAMPS VALID was stuck on all Jersey letter boxes.

When the British Government declared all Rhodesian decimal currency stamps invalid and charged double postage, the Jersey Post Office had to surcharge all letters bearing these stamps. Special labels were printed in black by the States Greffe reading 'The States of Jersey has announced that stamps issued in Rhodesia of the kind used on this postal packet have no legal status. This packet is accordingly surcharged'. Three different sizes of label were used and occasionally the red British Post Office labels were used on letters addressed to Jersey. Some of the letters also received the boxed STAMP INVALID mark.

After the British Government lifted the ban some letters received in September, 1970, had the postage due stamps cancelled with the old boxed mark used by the British Post Office CHARGE NOT COL-LECTED/FRESH LABEL REQUIRED with a large x in the centre.

The new status of Jersey and Guernsey as independent postal authorities has created a greatly increased demand for Channel Islands stamps and postal markings from all over the world. Philatelic Bureaux have been established in both islands. In Jersey the Bureau is at 6a Colomberie, St. Helier. The postal address is P.O. Box 304, St. Helier, Jersey. The Guernsey Bureau is at the Head Post Office, Smith Street, St. Peter Port. It is possible to leave deposits and standing orders for new issues with both bureaux. The service they both give is excellent and a standing order will enable one to keep up to date with all future issues. Both Postal Administrations publish regular Bulletins giving details of their stamps, stationery, and postal markings. These are available free upon request.

13

MISCELLANEOUS MATTERS

The Channel Islands Arms

A note on the Arms used on the Channel Islands stamps may be of interest to readers (Figure 13.1). The Arms came originally from the seal of Edward I, which was given to the islands in 1279 for sealing wreckage. This seal no longer exists but a wax impression is preserved in the National Archives, Paris. It bears the three lions passant guardant of England and the legend 'S. Ballivie Insularum pro Rege Anglie'. In 1302, when each island had its own Bailiff, separate seals were made, modelled on that of Edward I, bearing the following inscriptions: (Guernsey) 'S. Ballivie Insule de Gernereye'; (Jersey) 'S. Ballivie Insule de Jersie'. The Guernsey seal also bears a sprig above the shield, which is supposed to represent the badge of the Plantaganets.

The Arms were never intended to be used as those of the Bailiwicks, but they were never recalled and the Islanders' legal right to them has since been confirmed by the Privy Council when giving permission for their use on local coinage and flags.

13.1

The Local Issues

The local posts are an interesting part of the story of the carriage of mail in the Channel Islands. Much has been written about them in the philatelic press and they are all listed in the *Specialised Priced Catalogue of Channel Islands Stamps*. The Herm issues are fully dealt with in *The Island of Herm and its Posts*. It is only necessary, therefore, in this chapter to give an outline of the various services.

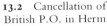

13.2 Cancellation of
British P.O. in Herm

13.3

HERM

Herm was the first of the small islands to issue local stamps. During the tenancy of Sir Percival (later Lord) Perry, from 1925 to 1938, there was a post office on the island which functioned as a sub-office of Guernsey (Figure 13.2). In 1945 the States of Guernsey purchased the island from the Crown and in 1948 leased it to a Mr. A. G. Jefferies. Mr Jefferies tried to get the sub-office re-opened, but the Head Postmaster of Guernsey refused on the grounds of insufficient business. Mr. Jefferies therefore decided to run his own service between Herm and Guernsey and had a series of five stamps prepared in 1948. Four values, ½d., 1d., 2d., and 6d., were for a boat service and a 1s. was issued for a pigeon service (Figure 13.3). They were all inscribed 'Postage', however, and were banned by the Postmaster General as an infringement of his monopoly. The stamps were issued on May 26, 1949, with the offending word blotted out.

The lease was sold to Major and Mrs. A. G. Wood, the present tenants, later in 1949 and they continued with local issues until these were suppressed by the Guernsey Post Office Board on September 30, 1969.

JETHOU

The next island to issue stamps was Jethou, half a mile from Herm. During the tenancy of Group Captain Headley Cliff the island was opened up to the public and in 1960 stamps were issued for the carriage of daily visitors' mail to Guernsey. The first series comprised five values, 1½d., 4d., 6d., 9d., and 18d. (Figure 13.4). Two designs featured the offshore islets of Crevichon and Fauconniere and carried

13.4

their names instead of Jethou. Other issues followed under Group Captain Cliff's tenancy and under that of Mrs. Susan Faed until they were suppressed by the Guernsey Post Office Board on September 30, 1969.

LIHOU

The little island of Lihou, owned by the Crown and leased to Lt. Col. Patrick Wootton, issued stamps in 1966–67 for the use of the daily visitors and the members of the youth camps held on the island (Figure 13.5). These, too, were suppressed on September 30, 1969.

13.5

BRECQHOU

The owner of Brecqhou, a small island off Sark, Mr. Leonard Matcham, planned a series of stamps for use on mail sent by himself and his staff, but these did not appear until September 30, 1969, and they were only used on that day as they came under the Guernsey Post Office Board's ban.

COMMODORE SHIPPING COMPANY

As mentioned in Chapter 7, from 1950 the Commodore Shipping Company Ltd., of Guernsey, issued adhesive labels for carriage of parcels to Sark by its vessels. The early labels were typeset, but from 1961 pictorials were issued (Figure 13.6). In 1962 separate issues were

13.6

made for carriage of parcels to Alderney. There was a genuine need for some of these issues, but others were made with one eye on the philatelic market.

The issues ceased on September 30, 1969, when the shipping contracts changed hands.

ALDERNEY SHIPPING CO. LTD.

On October 1, 1969, the Alderney Shipping Co. Ltd., of Guernsey, issued typeset labels in denominations of 2s. 3d. and 3s. for carriage of parcels to Alderney. These are still in use.

ISLE OF SARK SHIPPING CO. LTD.

On October 1, 1969, the Isle of Sark Shipping Co. Ltd. issued typeset labels in denominations of 1s. 6d., 2s., and 2s. 6d. for carriage of parcels to Sark. These are still in use.

SARK QUATERCENTENARY LABELS

In 1965 the Dame of Sark authorized the issue of pictorial labels (Figure 13.7) to commemorate the quatercentenary of the island's settlement. Although they bear denominations of 3d., 6d., 9d., and 1s. they performed no postal service.

13.7

The Revenue Issues

Jersey, Guernsey, and Alderney have each issued their own revenue stamps for stamp duties and legal charges. They are not subject to the British Stamp Duty Acts and they have their own Insular Insurance schemes.

JERSEY

On April 10, 1900, the States of Jersey passed a 'Reglement' which laid down a scale of Stamp Duties and necessitated the issue of revenue stamps. These were to have been issued on May 1, 1900, but as they had not been delivered by the printers by that date, resort had to be made to a local firm to produce some provisionals. Four hundred 1s. and 2s. 6d. stamps were printed on white wove paper,

13.8

perforated 12. They carried the inscription 'Etats de Jersey', the denomination and 'Tresorier', and were initialled 'H.N.G.', by the States Treasurer, Henry Nicolle Godfrey. Used copies are cancelled with a large purple handstamp with the States Arms in the centre (Figure 13.8).

A series of pictorial stamps from 1s. to £2 was issued on July 1, 1900. The designs were prepared by Wyon & Co., London, who ordered the stamps from De La Rue & Co. Ltd. They were printed on white wove paper, perforated 14½. The values were 1s. lake, Jersey Cow; 2s. green, Victoria College; 2s. 6d., purple, Mont Orgueil Castle; 5s. black, Arms of Jersey; 10s. blue, St. Helier's Harbour; £1 sepia, Copley's painting of the Battle of Jersey; £2 grey, Corbière Lighthouse. *See* Figures 13.9 and 13.10.

The set remains in use with the following alterations: the 5s. had the colour changed to vermilion in 1912 and the perforations were changed to 12. In 1922 two further denominations were added: £4 mauve, Ruined Arch of Gronez Castle; £10, chocolate, La Hougue Bie (both designed by Alan Wyon). In 1963 another two values appeared: £25 green, the Airport; £50 blue, Royal Square. Both

13.9

13.10

were perforated 12½. Other denominations are now also perforated 12½. The values up to 10s. have now been changed to decimal currency as follows: 5p., 10p., 25p., 50p.

During the German Occupation it was impossible to obtain the revenue stamps from London and locally printed 1s. and 5s. stamps were printed by Bigwoods, the States Printers, by making half-tone blocks from the London-printed designs. The local productions of 1942 were on white or grey paper roughly perforated 12. The 1s. is known as an imperforate-between horizontal pair.

In March, 1915, the States decided that all contracts for property should bear stamps to the value of 1s. for every £100 value of property. The proceeds were placed in a special fund to form a guarantee for 'rentes' created on property. The system of rentes is peculiar to Jersey and corresponds to a mortgage; however, unlike a mortgage, the owner cannot foreclose, but can only sell the rente on the open market. Until this fund was created a rente might be lost by virtue of the property so deteriorating as to become worth less than the value of the rentes upon it. By the creation of the special fund no rentes could be lost. Special stamps were created for these fees. There were five denominations in the same designs as the ordinary revenue stamps but triangular in shape: 1s. red, Jersey Cow; 2s. green, Victoria College; 5s. red, Arms of Jersey; 10s. blue, the Harbour; £1 sepia, the Battle of Jersey. The stamps exist perforated both 12 and 14½.

The revenue stamps from 1s. to £1, including the locally printed 1s. and 5s. of 1942 and the decimal 5p., 10p., and 25p., exist overprinted JURÉ JUSTICIER. These are for collection of fees due to the Jurats of the Royal Court for signing affidavits.

The island has had its own insurance stamps since 1936 when a 3d. red Social Assurance stamp was issued featuring the Arms of Jersey. It remained in use until 1951 when a new insurance scheme came into being. During the German Occupation a local printing of the stamp was made by Bigwoods by making a half-tone block of an original.

A series of small stamps of horizontal format, with the Arms of Jersey at the left and the denomination at the right was issued on September 10, 1951, for a new Insular Insurance. Denominations ranged from 1s. 3d. to 5s. 8d. A 1s. 5d. provisional was created in 1952 by surcharging the 1s. 3d. in large black figures. In 1954 a 3s.

was created by surcharging the 2s. 10d. Further series in a similar design were issued in 1961 and 1965. New denominations with overprint 'I.H.' (Insular and Health Insurance) were issued in 1967.

In December, 1968, a series of nine was issued surcharged with decimal equivalents of the denominations. A new series in decimal currency was issued on February 15, 1971.

GUERNSEY

Guernsey's Stamp Duty Law was sanctioned by an Order in Council dated August 10, 1903, registered on the Records of the States on August 29 and brought into force on October 29. This resulted in an issue of revenue stamps in denominations of 1d. mauve, 8d. green, 1s. 3d. vermilion, and 2s. 6d. ultramarine in large format depicting the Arms of Guernsey. They were printed by Waterlow & Sons Ltd. on white wove paper perforated 14. The Order in Council was amended in 1905 and the following additional values were issued: 6d. chocolate, 1s. deep orange, 1s. 8d. carmine.

All the above stamps were withdrawn on January 16, 1922, when the Order in Council was repealed. The 1d. was then re-introduced in a smaller size for use on receipts. Under the provisions of the Order in Council of March 7, 1931, the duty on receipts was raised to 2d. and a stamp of this value in a slightly modified design and in orange was issued (Figure 13.11). The 1d. remained in use and both were perforated 12½.

During the German Occupation the 1d. stamp was locally printed by the Guernsey Press Co. Ltd. It was made by photographing a normal stamp and making a half-tone block from it.

The 1903 1d. was overprinted 'STATES' for use on official receipts.

Examples of the 2d. can sometimes be found postally used during

13.11

13.12

the German Occupation, but it was never authorized.

In 1961 the stamp was printed by De La Rue from the Waterlow plate and in 1962 De La Rue made a new plate.

Revenue stamps were withdrawn on April 1, 1962, when the stamp duty on receipts was abolished.

Entertainments Tax stamps were printed by Waterlow in six denominations, ½d., 1d., 1½d., 2d., 2½d., 3d., and issued in 1919. During the German Occupation they were used for a few weeks as Sales Tax Stamps.

A Sales Tax Law came into force on August 21, 1940, and for this purpose a set of stamps was printed by the Guernsey Star Company Ltd. All the stamps were in shades of orange and the denominations were surcharged in black in various typefaces (Figure 13.12). The denominations were: ½d., 1d., 1½d., 2d., 2½d., 3d., 4d., 5d., 6d., 9d., 10d., 1s., 1s. 3d., 1s. 8d., 2s. 6d., 5s., 10s., £1, £5. They were issued in batches between August 21, 1940, and July, 1942. In January, 1946, the £1 and £5 were withdrawn because they were continually falling off invoices, etc., and being used over and over again, with a large loss to the revenue.

In 1946 a new series of stamps was printed by Waterlow. Each value was printed in red, with the Arms in the centre, and the denomination was surcharged in black (Figure 13.13). Values were: ½d., 1d., 1½d., 2d., 2½d., 3d., 4d., 5d., 6d., 9d., 10d., 1s., 1s. 3d., 1s. 8d., 2s. 6d., 5s., 10s. The stamps were withdrawn on August 31, 1947.

Income Tax stamps were printed by Waterlow in a design depicting the Arms of Guernsey and issued in April, 1947, in denominations of 1s., 2s. 6d., 5s., and 10s. (Figure 13.14). When De La Rue purchased Waterlow's in 1961 they took over the printing of these stamps.

13.13

13.14

On February 15, 1971, the Income Tax stamps were issued in decimal denominations of 25p., 50p., and £1.

Embossed revenue stamps were issued at the same time as the adhesives on October 29, 1903. Denominations were 1d., 8d., 1s. 3d., 2s. 6d., 3s. 9d., 5s., 6s. 3d., 7s. 6d., 10s., 20s., £5. These were embossed directly on to documents in vermilion ink.

The last issue was in different designs, with a different shape for each denomination. These were: 1d., 2d., 6d., 10d., 1s., 1s. 3d., 2s., 2s. 6d., 3s., 4s., 5s., 6s., 6s. 3d., 7s., 7s. 6d., 8s., 9s., 10s., 12s., 12s. 6d., 15s., 17s. 6d., £1, £2, £3, £5, £10, £25, £50, £100, £250. Each design had removable date plugs which gave the day, month, and year of striking. The 2d. was often struck on gummed, printed receipts in books.

There were also dies for the States of Guernsey Entertainments Tax.

Guernsey first issued insurance stamps in 1925 under the Workers' Accident Insurance Law which came into force on January 17. There were two values: 1½d. green (for females) and 3d. red (for males), inscribed 'Workmen's Compensation'.

In 1935 a Contributory Pensions Law brought into being a new scheme and new stamps inscribed 'Guernsey States Insurance— Accidents, Widows, Orphans, Old Age'. They were printed by Waterlow in denominations of 2d., 4d., 4½d., 8½d., 9d., 1s. 5d. During the German Occupation 4½d. and 9d. values were printed locally by the Guernsey Press Co. Ltd. from half-tone blocks of the originals.

New values were issued in 1947, 1956, 1958, 1960, and 1962. The 1962 issue was printed by De La Rue from the Waterlow plates. New plates were then made for the final printing in 1964.

A new Insurance Law came into force in 1965 and small horizontal-format stamps were issued on January 4, with the Arms at the right and the denomination at the left. Values ranged from 3d. to 9s. 4d. New printings and values appeared in 1967, 1969, and 1970.

A decimal/£sd. series appeared on September 7, 1970. It will be replaced by a decimal-only series when stocks are exhausted.

ALDERNEY

A single 1d. indigo revenue stamp was issued in Alderney in January,

 13.15

1923. It was printed by Waterlow and featured the Alderney Arms. This was replaced in 1931 by a 1d. red, which in turn was replaced in 1939 by a 2d. orange (Figure 13.15). A new printing was made in 1961 by De La Rue from the Waterlow plate. The stamp was withdrawn on April 1, 1962.

There was an oval embossed 2d. stamp with the Lion Rampant in the centre. For higher values Guernsey dies were used.

Private Cachets

There have been quite a number of private cachets used in the Channel Islands and many of these are of considerable interest to philatelists. A list of those known to me is given below.

ALDERNEY

1957. Visit of the Queen and Duke of Edinburgh, large boxed type in black.

1962. 577 (HAMPSHIRE)/FIELD SQN. R.E.(T.A.)(dated), boxed purple cachet of Territorial Army camp.

1962. 'Alderney THE Channel Island', green unframed cachet of States of Alderney.

GUERNSEY

1865. GOVERNOR/GUERNSEY, with Royal Arms surmounted by crown, blue oval cachet.

1871. EUGENE TILLOT/GUERNSEY, blue oval cachet.

1872. EUGENE CADIC/GUERNSEY with fleur-de-lis in centre, black oval cachet.

1905. ARMY PAY OFFICE/(DATE)/GUERNSEY, boxed violet type.

1907. COW LANE/ST. MARTIN'S/OLD GUERNSEY, black circular type. Used at Old Guernsey Fair, St. Martin's, on April 3, 1907.

1915. GREAT WESTERN RAILWAY/GUERNSEY, with AGENT'S OFFICE and date in centre, in blue oval.

1957. Visit of the Queen and Duke of Edinburgh, large boxed type in black.

1966. MAISON DE VICTOR HUGO & HAUTVILLE HOUSE, straight-line cachet in black.

1970. GERMAN MILITARY/UNDERGROUND HOSPITAL, with GUERNSEY in centre, dark blue oval type.

JETHOU

1909. JETHOU ISLAND/date (day and month only)/CHAN.ISLES, circular cachet in violet. Known on unused and used postcards. Possibly used on postcards sold on excursion steamer to Jethou. *See* Figure 13.16.

13.16

JERSEY

1843. A. EDOUARD LOZEY/JERSEY, in black oval.

1848. P. BEGHIN & CIE/NEGTS./A JERSEY, in black oval. Blue in 1850.

1872. W. T. PUGSLEY/SHIP & INSURANCE BROKER/ & COMMISSION AGENT/JERSEY, in large blue oval.

1893–1903. CONSULADO DE LA REPUBLICA DE COLOMBIA/JERSEY, with Colombian Arms in centre, large oval type in black or blue.

1904–05. HOTEL/de la POMME D'OR/JERSEY, unframed in black or blue.

1903–04. Grand Hotel du Palais de Cristal/J. PARISON Proprietaire/ JERSEY, ILES DE LA MANCHE, in very large purple oval with serrated border.

1908. MEDICAL CORPS/THE ROYAL MILITIA OF JERSEY between large double circle, with large cross in centre, in violet.

1908. ST.HELIERS/BAZAAR in large circle with SEP.1908 in centre, in violet (Figure 13.17).

1909. 'Grove Place/Wesleyan Bazaar/Aug.5,09', unframed in violet.

1911. HOTEL DE L'EUROPE/JERSEY, in violet oval.

1913. WOLF CAVES/ST. JOHN'S/JERSEY, in small double circle in violet.

1950s. THE MUSEUM/LIBRARY/JERSEY in black double circle with serrated border. Used by the Société Jersiaise. Still in use.

1957. Visit of the Queen and Duke of Edinburgh. Large boxed cachet in black.

1950s GERMAN UNDERGROUND HOSPITAL/JERSEY, in black or violet in large circle, open cross in centre with swastika in the middle. Still in use.

13.17

SARK

1957. Visit of the Queen and Duke of Edinburgh, large boxed type in black.

Maximum Cards

The Channel Islands were the only part of the British Isles to have accepted maximum cards until regulations were relaxed in 1970. These cards, which show a view or a portrait of a famous person or some other design similar to that featured on a stamp issue, have the stamp affixed to the picture side of the card and postmarked in the place depicted or the place associated with the person portrayed. Sets of them were sent through the post in Jersey and Guernsey during the German Occupation with the Arms stamps of both islands and with the views featured on the Jersey pictorial stamps of 1943. Although not actually permitted by postal regulations, they were freely accepted by the local post offices.

In 1953 a quantity of cards with portraits of the Queen and the Coronation stamps and Queen Elizabeth definitives also went through the Jersey post office.

The present Guernsey and Jersey Postal Administrations accept maximum cards for cancellation at their philatelic bureaux.

Maximum cards have been collected by Continental collectors for many years and have been accepted by most European post offices.

Unofficial Postal Service of the States of Guernsey

An interesting unofficial postal service in Guernsey has been running for many years on behalf of the States. Apology for absence forms from members of States Committees were marked with a printed inscription. Pink forms were inscribed POSTAGE WILL BE PAID ON DELIVERY TO THE STATES OFFICE, and blue forms POSTAGE WILL BE PAID ON DELIVERY TO THE STATES OFFICE ANNEXE.

It is not known when the service started, but it goes back to at least 1941. Some forms appear to have been delivered without any charge being collected but most carry postage due labels for double the deficiency.

The service still continues.

Jersey P.O.W. Camp, 1915

On March 20, 1915, a P.O.W. Camp for German prisoners was opened at Blanches Banques, Jersey. For a few weeks a large single-circle mark reading POST FREE/PRISONERS OF WAR/P.C. was applied in magenta or black to prisoners' mail. This was then replaced by a double-ring circular cachet with JERSEY at the top, CHANNEL ISLANDS at the bottom, and P.C. in the centre (Figure 13.18). This was the

13.18

censor mark of the camp and is found struck in red in April, 1915, and in violet in December, 1915. In addition, covers bear an oval stamp in black with PRISONERS OF WAR at the top, INFORMATION BUREAU at the bottom, and a crown in the centre; there is also the red London Official Paid datestamp.

Stamps Perforated with Initials of Firms

Some collectors like to include the security perforations of Channel Islands firms in their collections. Several Jersey firms perforated their stamps but so far no Guernsey one has been recorded.

By far the oldest Jersey firm to perforate its stamps is A. De Gruchy which uses a small DE in a large G (Figure 13.19). This has been used from about 1876 and the following stamps are known: 1858–64 1d. red, plates 180, 201, 222; 1881 1d. lilac; 1884 2½d. lilac; 1902 1d., 2d., 6d.; 1912–22 2d., 2½d.; 1936 1s.; 1936 Edward VIII 1½d.; 1938 1d. red; 1941 1d.; 1943 2½d.; 1948 Silver Wedding 2½d.; 1951 Festival of Britain 2½d.; 1952 ½d., 1d., 1½d., 2d., 2½d., 3d., 4d., 5d., 6d., 7d., 8d., 9d., 10d., 11d., 1s.; 1955 ½d., 1d., 2d., 3d., 4d., 5d., 6d., 8d., 10d., 11d., 1s.; 1953 Coronation 2½d.; 1957 Parliamentary 4d., and the 2½d., 3d., and 4d. Regionals. Others probably exist.

13.19

The Commercial Union used G.B. stamps perforated cu/s since November 1, 1953, in the following denominations: ½d., 1½d., 2d., 2½d., 3d.

The Automobile Association used British stamps perforated AA from June 1, 1948, to 1969 in the following values: ½d., 1½d., 2d., 2½d., 3d., 4d., 6d., 1s.

Fuel Supplies (C.I.) Ltd. used 1d., 2d., 2½d., 3d., and 6d. stamps perforated F S/LD in two lines from 1957 to 1969.

The perforation LMJ is known on a 1d. George VI stamp of 1938 but the Jersey firm to which it belongs has not yet been identified.

Other perforated stamps used in Jersey were the ½d. and 1d. Victorian stamps of 1887 with G.W.R. and L.S./W.R. of the Great Western Railway and the London and South Western Railway.

Some Victorian ½d. and 1d. stamps perforated J/EX and T &/W F have Jersey cancellations but it is not known whether they belonged to local firms or were used on stamped envelopes and postcards sent for reply.

Mystery Essay

The label illustrated in Figure 13.20 was produced in the 1860s in several colours. It has been claimed as an essay for Scotland but the Arms are wrongly quartered for Scotland, and the engraving gives the impression of local work rather than of a London printer. Could it have been produced as an essay for Jersey?

13.20

Reply Coupons

JERSEY

Reply Coupons, both Commonwealth and International, which can be exchanged for postage stamps equivalent to the single letter rate, were issued in Jersey on October 1, 1969. The Commonwealth Reply Coupon was inscribed JERSEY/CHANNEL ISLANDS and cost 7d. The International Reply Coupon was inscribed JERSEY, LES ILES DE LA MANCHE/JERSEY, CHANNEL ISLANDS and cost 1s. 3d.

On February 15, 1971, they were replaced by similar coupons with the selling prices indicated as 7d./3p. and 1s. 3d./6p. These in turn were replaced on July 1, 1971, by similar coupons inscribed 4p. and 10p. respectively.

GUERNSEY

Similar coupons were issued in Guernsey on October 1, 1969. The Commonwealth Reply Coupon was inscribed GUERNSEY/CHANNEL ISLANDS and sold for 7d. The International Reply Coupon was inscribed GUERNESEY, LES ILES DE LA MANCHE/GUERNSEY/, CHANNEL ISLANDS and was priced at 1s. 3d.

These were replaced on February 15, 1971, by identical coupons overprinted in violet with a rectangle containing a bar at the left cancelling the old value and the new value, 3p. or 6p., at the right. These in turn were replaced on July 1, 1971, by coupons inscribed 4p. and 10p. respectively.

British Postal Strike, 1971

During the British postal strike, from January 20 to March 7, 1971, there were a number of services carrying mail to the Channel Islands, but most of them did not run on a regular schedule. The services are as follows.

The Europa Mail Delivery, organized by D. Rosen & Son, 266 Pentonville Road, London, N.1. This service did a number of trips to both Jersey and Guernsey, posting letters on arrival. A 3s. 6d. red stamp reproducing the Occupation Jersey 1d. and Guernsey 2½d. stamps was issued on February 6, but the earliest covers seen that were actually carried and posted in the Channel Islands are dated February 12. Covers are known with this stamp used on either the front or the back. It is normally cancelled with a single-circle datestamp inscribed EUROPA/MAIL. Some covers addressed to Guernsey with the Europa Mail Delivery stamp on the front had the stamp blotted out with blue pencil by the Guernsey Post Office; others with the stamp on the back got through without difficulty.

On February 15 a 20p. green was issued in the same design. On the same day the 20p. was issued in red with black overprint '30th ANNIVERSARY/FIRST GUERNSEY STAMP/18th FEB. 1941'. This also appeared in the form of an imperforate miniature sheet. On February 18 some of these were posted in Guernsey and the Guernsey 2p. stamp received the special Guernsey commemorative cancellation.

The Bournemouth and District Emergency Postal Service, organized by Collectors' Corner, 190 Christchurch Road, Bournemouth. The 25p. stamp of this service was overprinted GUERNSEY diagonally in black and two copies (50p.) were used on a service to Guernsey via the mail steamer from Weymouth and posted on arrival, with a Guernsey 2½p. stamp.

Harmer's Post, organized by Sydney Harmer and Robert Ceram, Frittenden, Kent. This service organized a courier mail to Gatwick Airport, where letters were flown to Guernsey by B.E.A. and posted on arrival. The charge was 4s.

Pennycabs Delivery Service, organized by Pennycabs, Pennycome-quick, Plymouth. Mail was flown from Plymouth to Guernsey and posted on arrival. The charge was 10s. defrayed by a 10s. blue Pennycabs stamp.

N.W. London Postal Services, organized by A. Bhawan, 81 Walm Lane, London, N.W.2. Some letters were flown to Guernsey and posted on arrival. The charge was 12s., defrayed by 1s., 2s., 4s., and 5s. stamps of the N.W. London Postal Services.

B.E.A. Airway Letter Service. Letters were flown to the Channel Islands by British European Airways at a charge of 4s. (3s. 7d. Airway Letter stamp and 5d. G.B.) for collection on arrival. If posted on arrival they had to carry Guernsey or Jersey stamps.

Services from the Channel Islands to Britain. The postal services functioned normally in the Channel Islands, but there was no direct mail link with Britain. There was an air service to France, instituted on January 22, 1971, as part of a regular service following an agreement with the French Post Office. Letters for Britain were sent *poste restante* to Calais and were collected by the Exporters Letter Service and brought to London at a charge of 1s.

Letters were also brought to Portsmouth by the Alderney Pilots and delivered by the Gosport Strike Post.

The tenant of Lihou was also allowed to use his local stamps during the strike for a service to Britain. The letters were flown to Southampton Airport by Aurigny Air Services and collected by the Emergency Strike Post, Southampton, and brought to London where they were delivered by the Soho Post. The Lihou locals were also overprinted 'Postal Strike 1971' and surcharged with new values in decimal currency.

The Channel Islands Specialists' Society

In various parts of this book mention is made of the Channel Islands Specialists' Society. This Society was founded in 1950 as the Channel Islands Study Circle, but the name was changed to its present title in 1951. It started with about a dozen members but very quickly rose to sixty, at which figure it remained steady until about 1968 when the States of Guernsey and Jersey announced that they would be operating independent postal services from October 1, 1969. From that time it rose rapidly to its present total of over 350.

The Society is open to all who are interested in Channel Islands stamps, both postage and revenue, and postal history. A *Bulletin* is published every other month giving information on new stamps and postal markings and notes on new discoveries and auction realizations. The Society has also published a number of works on Channel Islands stamps and postal history and a *Specialised Priced Catalogue of Channel Islands Stamps.*

An exchange packet is circulated and an occasional postal auction is held. The Society does not hold general meetings at the present time because of its widespread membership and the difficulty of arranging a suitable meeting place, but some regional meetings have been held to give members in a particular locality an opportunity of contacting each other. Several members of the Society also give displays to philatelic societies up and down the country.

Membership details can be obtained from the Secretary, William Newport, 33 Halfway Street, Sidcup, Kent, England.

BIBLIOGRAPHY

General Works

R. C. Alcock and F. C. Holland. *The Postmarks of Great Britain & Ireland* (Cheltenham, 1940) and *Supplements*.

R. C. Alcock and F. C. Holland. *Maltese Cross Cancellations* (Cheltenham, 1959 and 1970).

O. G. Bowlby. 'Maritime Postal Markings', *The Philatelist*, November 1949.

H. L'Estrange Ewen. *Priced Catalogue of the Newspaper and Parcel Stamps issued by the Railway Companies of the United Kingdom, 1855–1906* (London, 1906).

Francis J. Field. *Airmails of the British Isles* (Sutton Coldfield, 1946).

A. Forbin. *Catalogue de Timbres Fiscaux* (Paris, 1915).

C. Grasemann and G. W. P. McLachlan. *English Channel Packet Boats* (London, 1939).

John G. Hendy. *The History of the Early Postmarks of the British Isles to 1840* (London, 1905).

John G. Hendy. *The History of the Postmarks of the British Isles, 1840–1876* (London, 1909).

Robson Lowe. *Encyclopaedia of British Empire Postage Stamps, Volume 1, Europe* (London, 1952).

P. L. Pemberton. 'British Stamps with French Postmarks', *Philatelic Journal of Great Britain*, July 1936, September 1936, December 1936, July 1937, July 1938, April 1939, June 1939.

Alan W. Robertson. *The Maritime Postal History of the British Isles* (Pinner, Middlesex, 1955).

Raymond Salles. *La Poste Maritime Française, Tome 1, Les Entrées Maritimes et Les Bateaux à Vapeur* (Paris, 1961).

Channel Islands

Baker's Catalogue and Handbook Stamps of the Channel Islands (Guernsey, 1943–49).

Ronald G. Burt. 'The Old Jersey Railways', *Bulletin of the Société Jersiaise*, 1961.

Yves Maximes Danan. *Émissions Locales et Affranchissements de Guerre des Iles de la Manche* (Paris, 1969).

D. V. Evans. 'Channel Is. Definitives Thick and Thin'. *Stamp Collecting*, vol. 115 (21 Jan. 1971) pp. 1257, 1259.

Richard Mayne. *Mailships of the Channel Islands 1771–1971* (Chippenham, 1971).

Heinz Möhle. *Kanal-Inseln Guernsey & Jersey, Deutsche Besetzung 1940–45* (Frankfurt, 1970).

William Newport. *The Channel Islands, their Postal History, Stamps and Postal Markings* (Birmingham, 1950).

William Newport. *Priced Catalogue of Channel Islands Revenue and Insurance Stamps* (London, 1952).

William Newport. *The Channel Islands—France Mails 1683–1939* (London, 1956).

O. W. Newport. *The Post in Alderney, Sark and the Chausey Islands and the Sub-Offices of Jersey and Guernsey* (London, 1956).

William Newport. *The Airmails of the Channel Islands* (Sidcup, 1957).

William Newport. *Early Channel Islands Postal History* (London, 1958).

O. W. Newport. *Priced Catalogue of Channel Islands Postal Markings* (Sidcup, 1965).

William Newport. *Specialised Priced Catalogue of Channel Islands Stamps 1971*, 6th edn. (Sidcup, 1970).

William Newport. *The Island of Herm and its Posts* (Sidcup, 1970).

O. W. Newport & O. J. Simpson. *The Datestamps and Other Cancellations of Jersey & Guernsey* (London, 1954).

William Newport and John Simpson. *The Numeral Obliterations and Instructional Marks of the Channel Islands* (London, 1956).

William Newport & John Simpson. *Postal Affairs During the German Occupation of the Channel Islands, 1940–45* (Sidcup, 1957).

O. W. Newport & O. J. Simpson. *Further Channel Islands Postal History* (Sidcup, 1961).

R. Northey. 'The Guernsey Tramway', *Transactions of the Société Guernesaise*, 1959.

J. M. Y. Trotter. 'Early Guernsey Postal History and Private Agents for Guernsey Letters', *Transactions of the Société Guernesaise*, 1950. *Postal History Society Bulletin*, 1950.

INDEX

Index

Index

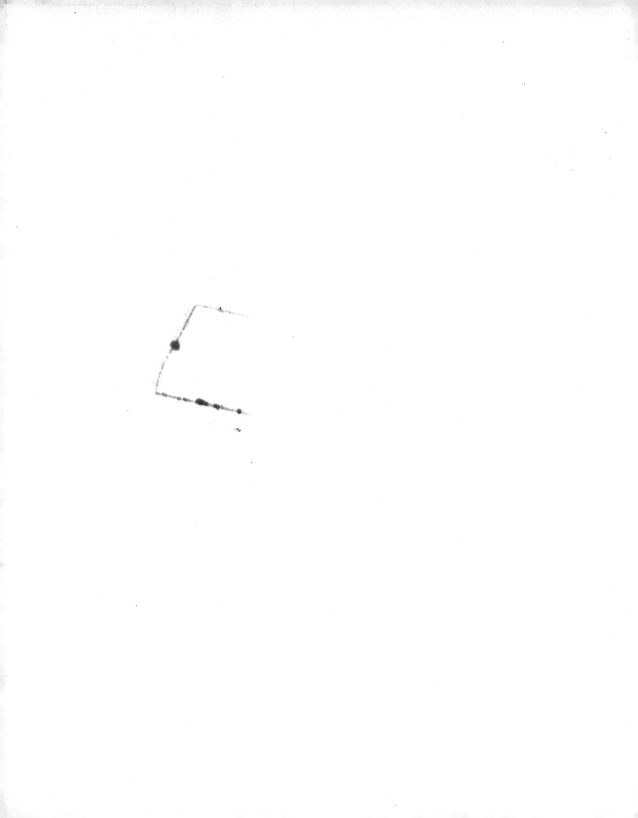